Images
of
Cornwall

Alan Bennett

DEDICATION

To Martin Mackenzie, Malcolm Jones and my wife, Jo, for 1991

Published by Runpast Publishing, 10 Kingscote Grove, Cheltenham, Glos
Printed by Amadeus Press Ltd, Huddersfield, West Yorkshire
© Alan Bennett/Runpast Publishing, 1992
ISBN 1 870754 22 0

INTRODUCTION

Cornwall is unique; it is Britain's most distinctive and best known county, the legendary land of Lyonesse, an ancient and mysterious place resonant of the past and rightly celebrated for its magnificent landscapes. The county's special identity, shaped also by mining and the sea, has made Cornwall the nation's most popular holiday area. Moorland, beaches, cliffs and the spectacular sea give it character and atmosphere not easily, if ever, surpassed elsewhere.

This book looks at three centuries of experience and event, each theme attempting to illustrate definitive features of the history, traditions and cultural identity of Cornwall and its people.

Alan Bennett
February 1992

ACKNOWLEDGEMENTS

I would like to thank the following people for their help and interest in the preparation of this book. Firstly, Stephen Mourton, who, as publisher, gave me the opportunity to develop the book, also, and always, Terry Knight, Joanne and Kim, at the Cornish Studies Library, Redruth, for their considerable assistance and ready cooperation. Thanks also to everyone at the magnificent Penzance Library, Morrab Gardens, Penzance, for the extended access to all-important records/reference materials and for some fine photographs. Roger Penhallurick of the Royal Institution, Truro, has been particularly helpful with regard to photographs; also to Mike Courtney of Courtwood Studios for rapid processing, to Peter Gray and, of course, Peter White for the cover and related help elsewhere in the book. Margaret Barron has, again, typed the script and coped with my often less than generous deadlines. Finally, I would thank my wife, Jo, for considerable help in all manner of ways, often when times were difficult. Thanks also to the boys, Robin and Che, for giving me peace and quiet at home.

Port Isaac on the North Cornish coast between Padstow and Tintagel. This traditional fishing community was destined to attract considerable interest from tourists with the opening of the LSWR North Cornwall line to Wadebridge in the summer of 1895. Padstow was not reached until 1899. In John Wesley's day Port Isaac proved to be receptive to his missionary work. Of Port Isaac in 1748 he wrote, "preached in the street to near the whole town, none speaking an unkind word – not five persons went away."

Cornish Studies Library

JOHN WESLEY AND CORNWALL IN THE EIGHTEENTH CENTURY

Between 1743 and 1789 John Wesley made a total of thirty-two visits to Cornwall. During that time, and in the face of often serious local opposition, he inspired fundamental change in the lives of many within the working community. Farm workers, fishermen and vast numbers of miners and their families were deeply moved by Wesley's message leading to the growth of the Methodist Movement, a powerful force in the social and cultural life of Cornwall.

Wesley's origins and early years, however, marked him out for a life-style and position far removed from that for which he became famous. One of a large family from the marriage of Samuel and Susannah Wesley, he was born at Epworth in Lincolnshire on 17 June 1703. His father, Samuel, was Rector of Epworth and a convinced High Church Tory; his mother, Susannah, was a deeply religious woman of very firm principles who ensured that the children grew up in an environment of devout faith, and strict personal discipline. Poverty and local hostility were all too apparent to the Wesleys at Epworth. Samuel Wesley had been imprisoned for debt, whilst the family, and their property, in particular, had been continually subject to physical attack, by sections of the local community. The children received their share of threats.

Wesley's early development most certainly had a profound influence upon him throughout his life. He never questioned his High Tory background, nor did he ever contemplate leaving the Church of England even when it opposed him so vehemently in his work as a preacher. The discipline, both mental and physical, exerted by his mother had an important bearing on his character. Wesley's seeming indifference to physical discomfort is well reflected throughout his 'Journal'. He travelled over a quarter of a million miles and preached over 40,000 sermons in the course of his work showing that neither illness, the elements nor age deterred him. Nor did the often extreme opposition that confronted him weaken his resolve once he discovered the exact nature of his work.

Susannah Wesley held the qualities of discipline and duty in high esteem. "In order to form the minds of children", she wrote, "the first thing to be done is to conquer their will and bring them to an appropriate temper." Her children were required to examine their consciences thoroughly and "when turned one year old they were taught to fear the rod and cry softly." At the age of five the Wesley children were set to learn sections of the Book of Genesis as a matter of course; a practice which went some way to explaining Wesley's remarkable memory. Play formed only the smallest part in Wesley's early life; discipline and study predominated, but there was no suggestion of unhappiness. At the age of eleven he attended Charterhouse and in 1720 entered Lincoln College, Oxford. Here he increasingly subjected himself to intense study and personal discipline, enduring considerable hardship and self-denial in pursuit of the highest standards of religious life, which he himself described as "personal holiness." Good works consisting of charity towards the poor and needy were also part of his life at this time. With colleagues in the 'Holy Club' he visited prisons and workhouses and provided food and clothing as well as elements of education to the poor. Wesley practiced strict austerity himself, cutting out all unnecessary material goods and giving money to those in need.

Whilst at Oxford he was deeply aware of the need to find a true vocation to give his life that vital sense of mission and purpose he earnestly desired. An early childhood experience, that of being saved from the disastrous fire which destroyed Epworth Rectory in 1709, had clearly inspired in him a belief in Providence, which never weakened. He was convinced that in having been saved he had been chosen for a special task, thus his tremendous sense of mission and endurance when, as a preacher, he faced vicious mob-rioting. In pursuit of his quest for purpose in life he left England in October 1735 for the American colony of Georgia. His intention was to become a missionary to the Indians, but this and an intense yet indecisive romantic involvement, brought him little fulfilment or purpose. Wesley left Savannah in December 1737, arriving back in England in February the following year painfully aware of his failure.

The great turning point for him came in May 1738, ten years after his ordination. On the 24th of that month he underwent his great conversion. Whilst listening to a reading from the 'Epistle to the Romans' at Aldersgate in London, Wesley later recorded: "I felt my heart strangely warmed, I felt I did trust in Christ, Christ alone for my salvation: And an assurance was given me, that he had taken away my sins, even MINE, and saved me from the law of sin and death." In March of the following year he began his famous work, being invited by George Whitefield, another extremely powerful preacher at that time, to preach to a gathering of miners at Kingswood, Bristol. Wesley responded to this challenge, recording his thoughts and feelings concerning it. In April 1739 he wrote: "I submitted to be more vile and proclaimed in the highways the great tidings . . ." Preaching to large gatherings in the open air, whether hostile or otherwise, was obviously a radical step for one of Wesley's background. In March 1739 he observed that: "having been all my life, till very lately, so tenacious of every point relating to decency and order, I should have thought the saving of souls almost a sin if it had not been done in church." He also claimed that, at first, "I could scarce reconcile myself to the strange way of preaching the fields." His tremendous energy and enthusiasm for his work, particularly his spirited appeal to the working population rapidly distanced him from the Church. Increasingly his style of preaching came in for severe criticism and he was, inevitably, banned from preaching in almost all churches including that at Epworth, his home. Wesley's response, was one of disappointment but also of resolve to continue despite the obstacles:

> "Seeing that I have now no parish of my own, nor probably ever shall, I look upon the whole world as my parish."

He then devoted himself for the rest of his life to his great work bringing the Word of God to all who would hear. In doing so he made close contact with the poor, particularly in the growing industrial areas, largely ignored by the Church of England. Counties such as Staffordshire, Derbyshire, Yorkshire, and, of course, Cornwall, became familiar territory for Wesley, appealing to people who, for the most part, lived in great neglect, spiritually and materially. Over his long career, Wesley focussed great time and effort on journeys to Cornwall, the first beginning on 29 March 1743 when, towards sunset, he and his companions crossed "the first great pathless moor beyond Launceston." His final visit ended on 28 August 1789, after having almost half a century of close personal contact with the county.

Wesley experienced considerable opposition during his early visits to Cornwall. The clergy and gentry generally set themselves against him, frequently inciting the common people to riot. Wesley was regarded with extreme suspicion during the early visits to the county. He was suspected of being a Jacobite, a supporter of the Catholic cause of Charles Edward Stuart, 'Bonnie Prince Charlie' to his followers, who, in 1745, with the help of the French planned an invasion of England, from Scotland. The 'Pretender' to the throne intended to drive out George II and restore the Stuart right to the crown. The French also planned an invasion of England as part of the overall campaign. Wesley was accused of being in direct support of the Catholic Stuart cause with several instances given where people, locally, claimed they had seen Wesley in France in the company of Charles Stuart. Adding to local tension at that time concerning the Stuart cause was the knowledge that a ship, the 'Elizabeth', carrying arms for the Jacobite army in Scotland, was engaged in battle by an English warship off the Lizard forcing the former to return, badly damaged, to France.

The Jacobite cause was destroyed for ever on the battlefield of Culloden in 1746, removing that particular charge against Wesley, but his direct appeal to the common people together with his style of field preaching still caused resentment. It was considered undignified and unworthy for someone of Wesley's position to indulge in such activities. Moreover, his appeal to the poor in particular was considered dangerous to society. It was feared that once this large but neglected section of society was encouraged to openly express a sense of awareness and identity, either individually or collectively, they would articulate their thoughts and ideas leading them on to unrest, and discontent, with their lot in life.

Despite all the various fears as to the nature and consequence of his work, Wesley was firmly committed to High Church Tory values. He exercised the strictest control over his followers insisting upon high standards of personal discipline and social obedience. It has been said of Methodism that it was primarily a religion for the poor, not one of the poor. Whatever the accuracy of such a statement, Wesley's emphasis upon discipline was a direct response to the social and economic conditions that he was well aware of around him. Eighteenth-century Cornwall was a particularly violent society. Lack of law and order, extreme punishments by way of deterrent, public hangings and floggings, brutal sports and pastimes, widespread drunkenness and all the extremes of riches and poverty made for circumstances where life was often brutal, short and, invariably, cheap. Wrecking and smuggling were two definitively Cornish activities that Wesley detested. In July 1753, for example, at St. Ives the 'Journal' records: "I found an accursed thing amongst them: well nigh one and all bought or sold uncustomed goods. I therefore delayed speaking to anymore till I had met them all together. This I did in the evening and told them plain either they must put this abomination away, or they would see my face no more." So much for smuggling; Wesley spoke with similar gravity concerning wrecking – the practice, locally, of plundering shipwrecks which, given the hostile coastline, were frequent occurrences. In August 1776 he described this activity as "the scandal of Cornwall" arguing that harsh measures should be taken against those taking part in order to set an example to the entire community. "Only Methodists," it was stated, "will have nothing to do with it."

The actual realities of smuggling and wrecking in the eighteenth century were far removed from much of the present day romanticism colouring notions of these and various other elements of life long ago. Both smuggling and wrecking were widespread in Cornwall giving rise to considerable concern; they also served to focus the problems of the deep divisions in society; the poverty and conspicuous wealth, and the difficulty in maintaining effective law and order which, of course, emphasised the obviously violent nature of the times.

Detailed correspondence maintained between George Borlase and Lieutenant General Onslow, in the early 1750s, served to destroy any heroic, romantic images surrounding the activities of the smugglers and the wreckers of West Cornwall. The letters also emphasise the highly organised and diffuse nature of these pursuits, by no means merely opportunist activities on the part of deprived people.

1 Febry 1753
George Borlase
to Lieut. Gen. Onslow.

The late storms have brought vessels ashore and some dead wrecks, in the former case great barbaritys have been committed, which a few soldiers would have prevented. And considering the coasts here swarm with smugglers from the Lands End to the Lizard, by which an immense sum goes yearly to France. I wonder they were ordered off without being replaced by others, as they are in those cases of great use.

Sir, I beg leave to present you my humble thanks for the continuance of the vote of your House. And with pleasure observe leave is given to bring in a Bill for enforcing the Laws against persons who shall steal or detain shipwrecked goods etc. A forfeiture of every man's wages due to him for any tin or copper mine who should leave his work to go a wrecking. And a clause for reading the Act in every Church and Chapel four times a year. A large penalty upon neglect of providing the Act and reading it would I apprehend greatly awe those brutes and have a very good effect.

15 March 1753
George Borlase
to
Lieut. Gen. Onslow.

As to soldiers I am sorry smuggling and wrecking are increased in those parts to such a degree as to render them necessary.

The riches of the land and sea is in full gallop to France and the countenance given to the smugglers by those whose business it is to restrain those pernicious practices both brought them so bold and daring that nobody can venture to come near to them with safety whilst they are at their work . . .

The people who make it their business to attend these wrecks are generally Tinners and as soon as they observe a ship on the Coast they first arm themselves with sharp axes and hatchetts and leave their tin works to follow the ships.

Sometimes the ship is not wrecked but where it is or not the mines suffer greatly not only by the loss of their labour which may be about £100 per diem if they are 2000 in quest of the ship where the water is quick the mine is entirely drowned and they seldom go in a less number than 2000.

Now tis hardly to be imagined how far the taking of this infamous practice in its very

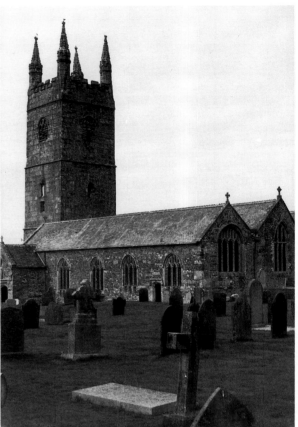

Three views of churches in North Cornwall where, in the early days, Wesley was welcomed as a preacher. Laneast (*top left*) was crowded exceedingly "to hear him, likewise, Tresmeer (*bottom*) was filled within and without while I preached." Week St Mary (*top right*) "the congregation was large, considering the weather, and quite attentive and unconcerned." Wesley's reception in West Cornwall was frequently very different with much opposition and organised disturbances during the early years. *Author*

bud and laying the loss of all wages due and some further penalty on every labouring tinner who should leave his tinwork in order to go to wreck would contribute to keep them home and break the neck of it.

The forfeitures would be certain loss, but the gain uncertain by going supposing no punishment attended their plundering.

Next I apprehend no person should be allowed to attend a wreck armed with axes or the like unless lawfully required. They will cut a large trading vessel to pieces in one tide and cut down everybody that offers to oppose them. Therefore there should be some provision against this.

Next I humbly apprehend the Bill does not sufficiently provide against the monstrous barbarity practiced by those savages upon the poor sufferers. I have seen many a poor man, half-dead, cast ashore and crawling out of reach of the waves fallen upon and in a manner stripped naked by those Villains, and if afterwards, he has saved his chest or any more clothes, they have been taken from him.

Inhuman and Barbaric as this is, and although a Highwayman is Christian to such I think whoever should forcibly take any goods out of the possession of such shipwrecked sailor by force should suffer as Highwaymen.

Helston and the surrounding district was said to be the centre, the most extensive and notorious in all the smuggling and wrecking activity of West Cornwall. In a further letter of 15 December 1750, George Borlase related how a Dutch ship of 250 tons, laden with claret was stranded near Helston and was thereupon stripped of its cargo by miners in less than 24 hours. In this instance the crew were saved.

Whatever Wesley's concern for order and discipline, his preachers were frequently the focus for local magistrates, eager to pronounce sentence against them. By no means the only instance was that of Thomas Maxfield. Arrested as a preacher, he was described by the authorities as having "no lawful calling or sufficient maintenance." The magistrates at Marazion accordingly, in June 1745, sentenced him to compulsory service for the King. Wesley records that Dr Walter Borlase and Mr Stephen Eustick, his two principal opponents in West Cornwall, had given orders to the local constables and overseers of the local parishes 'to apprehend all such able-bodied men.' The warrant, also included the names of seven or eight other people, whom, according to Wesley, " were well known to have lawful callings and a sufficient maintenance nearby. But that was all one: they were called Methodists; therefore soldiers they must be." Wesley was himself the subject of several attempts at arrest. Walter Borlase had made efforts to detain him at St Just; elsewhere, at Crown and Gwennap, other attempts were made, all without success.

By contrast, Wesley appeared to receive a warmer response in parts of North Cornwall. The Rev John Bennet at Tresmeer, for example, made his church available to Wesley, who frequently preached there to large gatherings, as was the case at Laneast, St Gennys and Week St Mary. In September 1748, Wesley wrote most favourably of his congregation at Tresmeer. "There was no need of speaking terrible things to these, a people ready prepared for the Lord." Similarly, at Camelford he noted that there were "none now offering to interrupt". At Port Isaac he "preached in the street to near the whole town, none speaking an unkind word. It rained most of the time, but I believe that not five persons went away." Six days later he preached at Newlyn in West Cornwall. "Here," he wrote, "was a congregation of a different sort, – a rude, gaping staring rabble-rout, some or other of whom were throwing dirt or stones continually."

In the face of considerable opposition Wesley always displayed great courage and determination. He confronted those who made it their business to disrupt or cause him actual harm, noting in his 'Journal' that he was often able to go a long way towards reasoning with his opponents quieting their anger, by fastening on to a particular individual. He certainly believed that his frequent escapes from the most dangerous riots were a direct result of Providence itself. At Walsall and at Falmouth, two of the worst riots he had to face in Britain, Wesley noted that "the hand of God was plainly shown him" by way of protection. The violence offered him at Walsall in the Midlands was particularly bad, this being in October 1743. The previous month saw trouble at St Ives. In this case it was evidently organised against him; Wesley, recording the incident, wrote, "Satan began to fight for his kingdom." The doors of the meeting house were broken down, members of the congregation were assaulted and

Above: Camelford, the small county town and gateway to the delights of Tintagel and the magnificent coastline of the fabled Lyonesse. In the days before the spread of the motor car, Camelford made an ideal centre for excursions across North Cornwall. As with many other locations within this area the people here many years before received John Wesley with great regard. Writing in his Journal for Sunday August 26 1750, Wesley wrote "Thence we hastened to Camelford where I preached in the main street, the rain pouring down all the time . . . Many were in tears and some could not help crying aloud." *Cornish Studies Library*

Left:
Activity in the street. St Ives, very early this century, with the inevitable cat in the foreground. The distinctive, narrow, cobbled streets familiar to Padstow, Newlyn or Looe, for example, gave Cornish fishing villages their obvious identity, and intense appeal for the tourist. St. Ives has been noted for its strong Methodist tradition, sometimes coming into conflict with its tourist image, but the Wesley's themselves faced serious opposition here during the 1740s. The town witnessed considerable unrest as, in Wesley's words, "Satan fought for his kingdom." *Cornish Studies Library*

Wesley himself was hit.

Wesley's brother, Charles, also had great difficulties at St Ives. In July of the same year, 1743, he described a particularly violent scene, by no means the only occasion, "I had just named my test at St Ives – when an army of rebels broke in upon us. They began in a most outrageous manner, threatening to murder the people if they did not go out that moment. They broke the sconces, dashed the windows in pieces, tore away the shutters, benches and poor box – They beat and dragged the women about and trampled on them without mercy." Eventually the rioters fell to quarrelling amongst themselves, finally breaking their leader's head and leaving. The leader proved to be the Town Clerk.

At Falmouth, in July 1745, Wesley was again in a position of great danger. Whilst visiting "a gentlewoman who had long been disposed," he wrote: "the house was beset on all sides by an innumerable multitude of people. A louder or more confused noise could hardly be at the taking of city by storm." The mob called for Wesley to be brought out, then they forced the door to the building, eventually breaking their way into the rooms themselves. Wesley confronted his attackers, but was soon after rescued by a Mr Thomas, a clergyman, and some gentlemen. Eventually in the face of increasing danger, Wesley was persuaded not to enter the streets again, but take the opportunity to make a judicious escape to Penryn by water. Wesley completed the record of this event with the following:

> I took boat at about half an hour past five. Many of the mob waited at the end of the town, who, seeing me escaped out of their hands could only revenge themselves with their tongues; but a few of the fiercest ran along the shore, to receive me at my landing. I walked up the steep, narrow passage from the sea, at the top of which the foremost man stood. I looked him in the face, and said, "I wish you a good night." He spoke not, nor moved hand or foot till I was on horseback . Then he said, "I wish you was in hell," and turned back to his companions.

That same evening whilst preparing to preach at Wendron, Wesley was subjected to another of the attempts to arrest him. In possession of a special warrant from the Justices at Helston, the church-wardens, constables and all the heads of the parish were awaiting him. In this instance, the vicar of Redruth took Wesley's part enabling him to avoid any further incident.

Organised opposition brought no reservation and no fears concerning his work, and general welfare; Wesley was not intimidated nor in any way deterred from his mission. Natural obstacles, of which there were many, were similarly , dismissed. Two entries in his 'Journal', one for September 1743, the other for April of the following year, illustrate the disregard of danger and extreme discomfort, emphasising his resolute, tenacious spirit.

Monday September 12 ....

> I had had for some time a great desire to go and publish the love of God our Saviour, if it were but for one day, in the Isles of Scilly: And I had occasionally mentioned it to several. This evening three of our brethren came and offered to carry me thither, if I could procure the Mayor's boat, which, they said, was the best sailer of any in the town. I sent, and he lent it me immediately. So the next morning, Tuesday, 13, John Nelson, Mr. Shepherd, and I, with three men and a pilot, sailed from St. Ives. It seemed strange to me to attempt going in a fisher-boat, fifteen leagues upon the main ocean; especially when the waves began to swell, and hang over our heads. But I called to my companions, and we all joined together in singing lustily and with a good courage:
>> When passing through the wat'ry deep,
>> I ask in faith his promis'd aid;
>> The waves an awful distance keep,
>> And shrink from my devoted head;
>> Fearless their violence I dare:
>> They cannot harm, – for God is there.

About half an hour after one, we landed on St. Mary's, the chief of the inhabited islands.

> We immediately waited upon the Governor, with the usual present, viz., a newspaper. I desired him, likewise, to accept of an 'Earnest Appeal.' The Minster not being willing I should preach in the church, I preached, at six, in the street, to almost all the town,

and many soldiers, sailors, and workmen, on, 'Why will ye die, O house of Israel" It was a blessed time, so that I scarce knew how to conclude. After sermon I gave them some little books and hymns, which they were so eager to receive, that they were ready to tear both them and me to pieces.

For what political reason such a number of workmen were gathered together, and employed at so large an expense, to fortify a few barren rocks, which whosoever would take, deserves to have them for his pains, I could not possible devise: But a providential reason was easy to be discovered. God might call them together to hear the Gospel, which perhaps otherwise they might never have thought of.

At five in the morning I preached again, on, 'I will heal their backsliding; I will love them freely.' And between nine and ten, having talked with many in private, and distributed both to them and others between two and three hundred hymns and little books, we left this barren, dreary place, and set sail for St. Ives, though the wind was strong, and blew directly in our teeth. Our pilot said we should have good luck, if we reached the land; but he knew not Him whom the winds and seas obey. Soon after three we were even with the Land's End, and about nine we reached St. Ives....

The second entry marks the beginning of his second visit to the county, describing the problems of bad weather and of losing direction in an often hostile landscape:

Monday April 2 ....

I preached at five, and rode on towards Launceston. The hills were covered with snow, as in the depth of winter. About two we came to Trewint, wet and weary enough, having been battered by the rain and hail for some hours. I preached in the evening to many more than the house would contain, on the happiness of him whose sins are forgiven. In the morning Digory Isbel undertook to pilot us over the great moor, all the paths being covered with snow, which, in many places, was driven altogether too deep for horse or man to pass. The hail followed us for the first seven miles; we then had a fair though exceeding sharp day. I preached at Gwennap in the evening to a plain simple-hearted people ...

Left: Digory and Elizabeth Isbel's cottage at Trewint immediately east of Bodmin Moor, near Launceston. Wesley stayed here, preaching on many occasions. The house was extended and adapted for the convenience of the preachers, making it a focal point in the early years of Methodist mission. The extension of one upper and lower room provides an obvious link with this past, and for the atmosphere and experience is well worth visiting. *Right:* Altarnun Church. Digory and Elizabeth Isbel are buried here in the churchyard. The inscription on the railed tomb reads: "They were the first who entertained the Methodist Preachers in this County."

Author

By the 1770s, Wesley was well received. He recorded that he could preach in any part of St Ives, and that, at Falmouth, larger crowds were gathering to hear him than had set in against him 25 years earlier.

Gwennap Pit, a focal point for Cornish Methodism, became a favourite location for his preaching from 1762 onwards. He wrote in the 'Journal' for 5 September that year:

> At one I preached in the main street at Redruth, where rich and poor were equally attentive. The wind was so high at five that I could not stand in the usual place at Gwennap. But at a small distance was a hollow capable of containing many thousand people. I stood on one side of this amphitheatre toward the top with the people beneath and on all sides, and enlarged on those words in the Gospel for the day . . .

Wesley also wrote of Gwennap Pit and of his congregation in September 1775:

> I think this is the most magnificent spectacle which is to be seen on this side of heaven. And no music is to be heard upon earth comparable to the sound of many thousand voices, when they are harmoniously joined together singing praises to God and the Lamb.

Gwennap Pit assumed much of its present appearance from 1806 when it was extensively improved by providing rising terraces of circular seating, the entire site being enclosed by a circular stone wall with gates giving access. It was reopened following the improvements at a special service at Whitsun 1807.

The numerous chapels which form such a distinctive part of the Cornish landscape testify to the active presence of the Wesleys throughout the county. Wherever possible he arranged for his meetings to be held at times unlikely to clash with the church and its services to avoid any element of competition. He had no intention of breaking away from the Church of England himself, and it was only after his death that Methodism emerged as a separate sect outside of the Established Church. Without doubt, he and his brother, Charles, responsible for many of our best known hymns, brought about a transformation in the lives of large numbers of people in Cornwall as elsewhere. According to Dr Paris writing on Penzance and the West Cornwall area in 1816, Methodism had brought about significant changes within the community:

> The Methodists in Western Cornwall are very numerous, and of a respectable description; and the change which they have effected in the morals of the miners is really incredible, and the habits of sobriety and order which they have happily introduced, have tended as much to the mining interests as to the quiet and comfort of the neighbourhood.

Roseworthy Chapel, still to be seen today on the south side of the road between Connor Downs and Camborne in West Cornwall. This photograph from the early years of the century shows the chapel in excellent repair and very much a focal point of this small community. Methodist chapels were a feature of Cornish towns and villages, as, indeed, they are today. Not all, however, were as interesting as this elegant thatched structure. The majority of chapels, many now abandoned, or converted for other purposes, were of sturdy Cornish granite, resilient but unflattering in appearance. *Cornish Studies Library*

Two views of Gwennap Pit at the turn of this century. It is one of the great focal points of Methodism in Cornwall and took on this appearance after Wesley's death. Opened as seen here at Whitsun 1807 it accommodated over 2000 people. Wesley considered the experience of preaching at Gwennap as "the most magnificent spectacle which is to be seen on this side of heaven." The second photograph shows the vast gatherings that characterised the meetings at Gwennap. *Royal Institution of Cornwall*

After almost half a century in which he made remarkable progress, despite the often determined opposition of both man and nature, Wesley undertook his final journey to the county in the latter part of August 1789. One year earlier, on June 28, 1788, Wesley considered his health and ability, explaining the circumstances:

Saturday 28 ...

I this day enter on my eighty-fifth year: And what cause have I to praise God, as for a thousand spiritual blessings so for bodily blessings also! How little have I suffered yet by 'the rush of numerous years'! It is true, I am not so agile as I was in times past. I do not run or walk so fast as I did; my sight is a little decayed; my left eye is grown dim, and hardly serves me to read; I have daily some pain in the ball of my right eye, as also in my right temple (occasioned by a blow received some months since), and in my right shoulder and arm, which I impute partly to a sprain, and partly to the rheumatism. I find likewise some decay in my memory, with regard to names and things lately passed; but not at all with regard to what I have read or heard, twenty, forty, or sixty years ago; neither do I find any decay in my hearing, smell, taste or appetite (though I want but a third part of the food I did once); nor do I feel any such things as weariness, either in travelling or preaching: And I am not conscious of any decay in writing sermons; which I do as readily, and I believe as correctly, as ever.

To what cause can I impute this, that I am as I am? First, doubtless, to the power of God, fitting me for the work to which I am called, as long as He pleases to continue me therein; and, next, subordinately to this, to the prayers of his children.

May we not impute it, as inferior means,

1.) To my constant exercise and change of air?

2.) To my never having lost a night's sleep, sick or well, at land or at seas, since I was born?

3.) To my having sleep at command; so that whenever I feel myself almost worn out, I call it, and it comes, day or night?

4.) To my having constantly, for above sixty years, risen at four in the morning?

5.) To my constant preaching at five in the morning, for above fifty years?

6.) To my having had so little pain in my life, and so little sorrow, or anxious care?

Even now, though I find pain daily in my eye, or temple, or arm; yet it is never violent, and seldom lasts many minutes at a time.

At the advanced age of 86 he was still actively engaged in his work. Recording the events of each day in the 'Journal', he wrote on Sunday 23 August of his final visit to Gwennap Pit, preaching there in the evening: "I suppose for the last time; for my voice cannot now command the still increasing multitude." That same morning he preached at Redruth, and on the previous day also, addressing "a huge multitude, as usual from the steps of the market house." Throughout the final visit lasting from Monday 17 to Friday 28 August he was extremely well received everywhere, claiming on 22 August, "I know not that I ever spent such a week in Cornwall before." At Falmouth, for example, he recorded "High and low now lined the street from one end of the town to the other, out of stark love and kindness, gaping and staring as if the King were going by." At Helston he preached in the High Street at noon on 19 August, observing that the congregation was the largest and most serious that he could ever remember in the town. Similar favourable reports were also to apply for Penzance, Newlyn, St Just and St Ives. The final entry in the 'Journal' for Cornwall came on Friday 28 August:

I preached at nine in our new house at Camelford, thoroughly filled, though at a short warning; and at six in the evening in the new house at Launceston, still too small for the congregation who seemed exceedingly lively. So there is a fair prospect in Cornwall, from Launceston to the Land's End.

Wesley continued his work elsewhere in England for a further eighteen months. He eventually returned to London, where he died on 2 March, 1791.

The widespread influence of Methodism during the nineteenth century was well reflected in the numerous chapels and societies established throughout Cornwall. Wesley had a profound impact upon the working people, in particular amongst the fishing and mining communities, and it is to the latter that we turn now, looking in detail at the daily life and labour of the miner and his family.

John Wesley in the closing years of a long and eventful life. This imposing and extremely dignified portrait expresses the sense of purpose, strength of character and resolution that defined Wesley's life and work.   *Royal Institution of Cornwall*

ST. JUST CIRCUIT.				
Name of Chapel.	Where situate.	When built.	Number of Sittings.	Members of Society 1876.
St. Just	St. Just	1832	1900	656
Trewellard	,, ...	1832	600	130
Buryan	Buryan	1832	320	48
Borah...	,, ...	1815	122	39
Crowsanwray	,, ...	1832	100	18
Sancreed	Sancreed	1823	172	79
Morvah	Morvah	1866	156	71
Bosullow	Madron	1815	220	63
St. Levan	St. Levan... ...	1869	220	104
Sennen	Sennen	1835	142	21
Newbridge... ...	Sancreed	1840	126	41
Nanquidno... ...	St. Just	1833	120	46
Dowran	,, ...	1840	90	50
Botallack	,, ...	1844	90	116
Bojewyan	,, ...	1841	130	49
Brea (House)	,, ...	—	30	15
Treen...	St. Levan... ...	1834	165	11
SEVENTEEN CHAPELS...			4703	1557
				In 1877, 1503

ST. IVES CIRCUIT.				
Name of Chapel.	Where situate.	When built.	Number of Sittings.	Members of Society 1876.
St. Ives	St. Ives (town)	1785	1200	236
Lelant	Lelant	1834	382	70
Carbis Water	,, ...	1841	120	36
Halsetown... ...	St. Ives	1832	320	28
Towednack	Towednack ...	1845	200	22
Nancledra	,, ...	1845	200	37
Polpear	Lelant	1873	110	21
Lelant Downs ...	,, ...	1843	120	32
Canons-town	Ludgvan	1839	110	28
Zennor	Zennor	1865	230	19
Porthmear... ...	,, ...	1839	100	22
Trendrine	,, ...	1845	100	8
Hallesveor... ...	St. Ives	1844	120	29
THIRTEEN CHAPELS			3312	588
				In 1877, 854

Mousehole – a typical Cornish fishing village, famous for being the victim of the Spanish raid of July 1595. Mousehole, nearby Paul, Newlyn and Penzance were all looted and burned by the Spaniards. Tourism is now the mainstay of this former fishing community which grew out of its close, perhaps, total identity with the sea; by no means always to its advantage. Mousehole suffered deep tragedy in December 1981 when the crew of the Penlee Lifeboat were lost at sea whilst answering the call of a ship in distress. This view from the mid 1920s shows the village before the onset of intense tourist activity. Fishing communities like this, around the Cornish coast, proved to be strong centres of Methodism from the eighteenth century. Wesley recorded the incidence of a water-spout at Mousehole in 1760. *Cornish Studies Library*

Methodist Chapels in West Cornwall in 1879

THE MINING COMMUNITIES:
THE NINETEENTH CENTURY EXPERIENCE

The Cornish landscape and parts of West Devon, along the Tamar Valley, offers extensive evidence of a rich and powerful industrial past, closely tied to the nineteenth century and to mining. Numerous engine houses of the former tin and copper mines stand empty and largely ruinous today, home now, not to the mighty steam engines that powered the mines, but to countless birds and animals. Dignified by silence and setting, softened by the process of nature and safely distanced through time, these are places resonant of the past, romantic and immensely appealing, yet far removed from their original, practical purpose. Such landscapes rarely fail to impress, but the serious focus and drama in mining was below ground. Unseen and inaccessible, the endless miles of underground workings that once yielded their massive mineral wealth are now flooded and largely forgotten; the focus of an industry and way of life that has vanished.

Copper mining, in particular, generated vast wealth, far greater than tin. It sustained entire communities and gave rise to important developments in transport and related trades, but was always a way of life fraught with danger, hardship and distress. Each day, as a matter of course, the miner faced the prospect of serious injury or death, perhaps by drowning, from subsidence, from explosion or a fall from a ladder in the darkness of an awkwardly aligned shaft. There was also the long-term threat; the insidious creeping death of the dust and damp; of consumption and chronic bronchitis.

Serious accidents or the death of a miner could also involve dire long-term consequences for his family, reaching beyond the sense of immediate personal tragedy. Deprived of the means of alternative financial support, a miner's family would certainly face the spectre of the workhouse and the stigma of pauperism. There was also the threat of collective distress within the wider community. The highly speculative nature of mining, the dependence upon the markets in terms of trade, prices and costs; upon the vital factors of effective management and investment, and inevitably the finite resources of the workings themselves underlined the fact that security, in its widest sense, could never be taken for granted. The mines maintained entire communities and determined their fate. For all these reasons, the mining population provided a forceful example of individuals, families and entire communities living on the edge.

The main mining districts of the South West working westward were: the Tamar Valley setts, including the phenomenally successful Devon Great Consols; the Caradon district, centring on Liskeard; the St Agnes-Perranporth district, along the North Coast, and inland, into mid Cornwall, the fabulously rich Gwennap district with the mighty Consolidated and United setts yielding vast fortunes. There were also the Camborne and Redruth districts, the heartland of Cornish tin and copper production, and the St Just district, in the far West, where mining was carried out beneath the sea bed. Helston, St Ives and the St Austell areas also had a number of mines, the latter including the rich Fowey Consols sett, near St Blazey.

Cornish copper production peaked in 1856 at a figure of 209,305 tons, thereafter figures for copper ore fell gradually to 1862, and then collapsed, bringing disaster upon the community. The fatal combination of large-scale foreign competition offering cheap imports and the mounting costs of production at home made it impractical to continue. Prices and production fell together. Copper was valued at £129 per ton in 1855; by 1870 it was worth only £72 13s per ton. For some thirty years prior to its terminal decline, however, copper mining enjoyed unprecedented success. Over a long, and at times, erratic period, reaching from as early as 1815 to 1856, the great Consolidated Mines at Gwennap produced some 441,286 tons of copper ore; neighbouring United Mines produced 347,640 tons. Gwennap, prior to the rise of these great copper concerns, was no more than a scattered, thinly-populated parish, supporting some mining and limited agriculture; by 1841 and the heyday of copper, the parish had a population of 10,794. Only Truro, the cultural and commercial capital of the county, (but not the county town) had a greater population.

Cornwall was undoubtedly the richest copper producing county in Britain, but the greatest output of copper ore from any one particular mining sett came from Devon Great Consols, immediately east of the River Tamar. A detailed survey of these workings offers an insight into the scale of copper mining in the nineteenth century, the nature of the work involved, and the enormous profits that were to be made, the latter bringing the situations of shareholder and employee into sharp relief.

Devon Great Consols Mine

Devon Great Consolidated was by any standards a rich and famous mining sett. Over the period 1844-1872 alone it raised ore to the value of £2½ million with £1 million being distributed in dividends to the shareholders. Its largest return in any one year to closure in 1903 was 28,836 tons of copper ore sold for £159,432, this being in 1857. Copper was its primary concern, but arsenic production was also important from the 1860s.

The mines making up Devon Great Consols were, individually, Wheal Maria, Wheal Fanny, Wheal Anna Maria, Wheal Josiah, Wheal Emma, and, to the south nearer the Tamar, Wheals Frementor and Thomas. On a wooded site north and east of the winding River Tamar, and west of the Tavistock-Gunnislake road, the mines marked the western extremity of the county, 3 miles west of Tavistock. Certain lodes ran westward under the Tamar itself and into Cornwall. (See Plans) All the land worked by these mines was owned by the Duke of Bedford who, despite the royalties coming his way, was said to have 'no great favour for these burrowings under the ground, as he considers the occupation of reaping the fruits of the earth above the surface to be more important.' *The Mining Journal* recorded in 1850:

> His grace is of the opinion that mining operations spoil his land and interfere with agricultural pursuits. The Duke's predecessor would have no interference with the land tolerating no gang of miners disturbing his pheasants.

Josiah Hugo Hitchens of Tavistock was from the outset convinced of the riches that lay underground, east of the Tamar. As a formative influence in the development, he drew attention to the prospect of handsome profits, attracting investment from London. In a letter of January 1844 he wrote on the subject: 'With respect to this property, I have only again and again to repeat that it is abounding, to a dead certainty, in metalliferous mineral deposits and resources – Let us have but a fair capital wherewith to bring them into operation and it cannot fail to be rendered capable of great results.' The Duke granted permission to work the land on a 21 year lease at ¹/₁₅ dues with the provision that as soon as profits reached £20,000 these dues be increased to ¹/₁₂. The capital raised for the venture amounted to £1,024.

Mining began at North Bedford, soon to be renamed Wheal Maria, in August 1844. This working, now named after Josiah Hitchen's wife, was soon to be successful. After several encouraging communications Hitchens wrote the following from Tavistock on 13 November 1844:

> I told you long since that we might expect something good before long, and now let me enjoy the pleasure of realising my anticipations. Last evening the lode began to assume a more decided character, although it had for many days previously exhibiting all the characteristics, having a tendency to the successful charge for which I have now the happiness to announce to you. The lode is now about 4 feet wide and excellent work it is, and we are now saving some for dressing, towards our first sampling, which I hope will be a good ore. The lode appears to be coming better and better every inch that is sunk in the shaft. – There is no fear in saying that as the lode is at present in the bottom of the shaft (now 17½ fathoms from the surface) it is worth £30 per fathom.

In the report of 26 December he was able to state:

> The lode, taking the length and width of the shaft 10 feet by 6 feet may be fairly reckoned as being worth at least £1,000 per fathom. We shall sample a small parcel tomorrow at Morwellham. Wheal Maria is all the cry – never was there such a wonderful discovery!

January 1845 saw the company designated 'Devonshire Great Consolidated Copper Mining Company'. Two months later Wheal Josiah began work, increasing output to the extent that the balance sheet for the year ending 31 January 1846 showed a profit of £73,622 17s. 1d. By this time an original £1 share in the mine was worth a staggering £800!

John Murcison, writing in *The Mining Journal* of 1850, gave a detailed account of developments at the mines. he was clearly impressed with the scale of operations and the success that had been achieved. Of the workings themselves he wrote:

> Notwithstanding the large profits divided in the year ending 31 March 1846, the expenses at the mines were necessarily very large. A water engine, (waterwheel) 24 feet diameter and 4 feet breast, with the requisite rods and jumps was erected at Wheal Maria. Two powerful and first rate water wheels, one for the purpose of grinding and

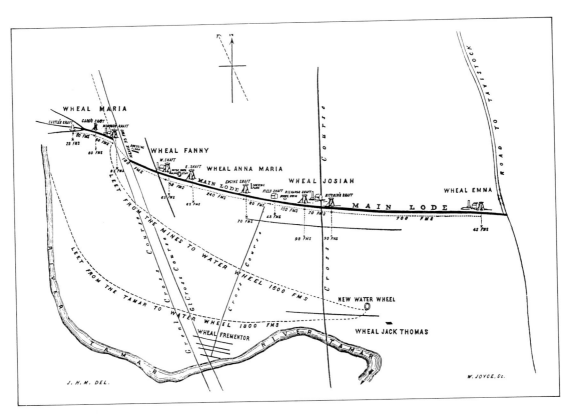

One of the very few photographs to have emerged of Devon Great Consols. It shows a general view of Wheal Emma, one of the many setts on this greatest of copper mines from the nineteenth century. Almost nothing survives today other than burrows and isolated sections of masonry, the site being returned to woodland and the preserve of wildlife, as it was before the development of mining in the 1840s.

Royal Institution of Cornwall

stamping and the other for hauling were nearly ready for erection. Another steam engine of 40 inch cylinder had also been delivered on the mine and the engine house was in active progress. A large and commodious counting house with all the conveniences of offices and changing rooms for the company's agents, extensive stables for the company's horses, immense workshops for their engineers, blacksmiths, carpenters, sawyers, and shaft and timber were built; and in every direction the best possible roads were made, in order to facilitate the transit of ores to their place of shipment. The roads required to be cut, made good and kept in repair, costing the company considerable outlay. The same requirements were carried out (1845) at Wheals 'Josiah and Fanny' – the latter being a new shaft sunk at a distance of 160 fathoms from Wheal Maria. In addition to its other machinery, a first rate water engine, with powerful crushing apparatus was erected. At Wheal Josiah, also, in addition to the machinery, expensive buildings, workshop premises and surface arrangements generally, a most perfect and powerful steam engine was erected. (This was another 40 inch cylinder engine similar to that at Wheal Maria. Work had also begun at this time at Wheal Anna Maria, named after her Grace the Duchess of Bedford, and at Wheal Frementor and Wheal Thomas, the two latter workings being south of the main lode close to the Tamar).

In the 12 months, ending 30 April 1847, the extent of drivage and exploration was costed at £3,738 1s.4d. – I should also observe that the ground mostly so soft and the lode so large, being sometimes as wide as 40 feet, and the average being 24 feet, that great quantities of timber were consumed for timbering the mine. A contract had been entered into in 1845 for 2,500 loads, and during the year ending April 1847 the sum spent for this article was £5,426 12s.10d. (Timber imports for the period January to December 1847 increased at a cost of £7,628).

At Wheal Maria a water engine of 50 feet diameter and 4 feet breast was erected by which at least £60 a month was saved in drawing ore alone. The dressing floors at this mine were much extended. Extensive dressing floors were also erected at Anna Maria, to which all the ore raised at Wheal Josiah, a distance of 210 fathoms is brought down by means of a self-acting plane – being a double tramway on which empty wagons are moved by the weight of those that are loaded as they descend.

A very important and valuable discovery was made at a distance of about 700 fathoms from Wheal Josiah, and nearly 120 fathoms from the eastern boundary of the sett. The operations on this extraordinary lode now extend from east to west for a distance upwards of 1400 fathoms. At a point where this new discovery was made, the lode was opened upon for about 60 fathoms and a shaft sunk to give effective trail to the concern. This mine was named 'Wheal Emma' in compliment to the widow of the late Mr William Morris, board member of the company.

The increasing depth of the mines requiring more powerful machinery, it was decided to adopt water power in preference to steam. For this purpose a grant of the use of the water of the Tamar was obtained from the Duchy of Cornwall at an annual rent of £250.
Devon Great Consols made full use of the water power now made available to them by constructing an extensive system of leats bringing water from the Tamar and from workings at the mines themselves. Murchison described the new water wheels and extensive supply leats:

The shaft at Anna Maria is drained by the new water wheel (1849) which also drains the two shafts at Wheal Josiah. . . The new water wheel is an object of great attraction at these mines. It is placed at the bottom of a hill, at a distance of about 390 fathoms from Richards' Shaft (Wheal Josiah) and about 64 fathoms below it . . . It gives about 150 horse power and is 40 feet in diameter and 12 feet breast (axle). It is connected with Richards' shaft by means of very strong flat rods working upon rollers on the top of very substantial (timber) supports.

It drains Richards', Hitchens' and Anna Marias' shafts. The water is brought about two miles from a point up the river in order to get the proper fall by a leat, (a weir on the river ensured a good supply) and the water pumped out of the mines and operating the crushing wheels and all other necessary work is brought round by another leat to

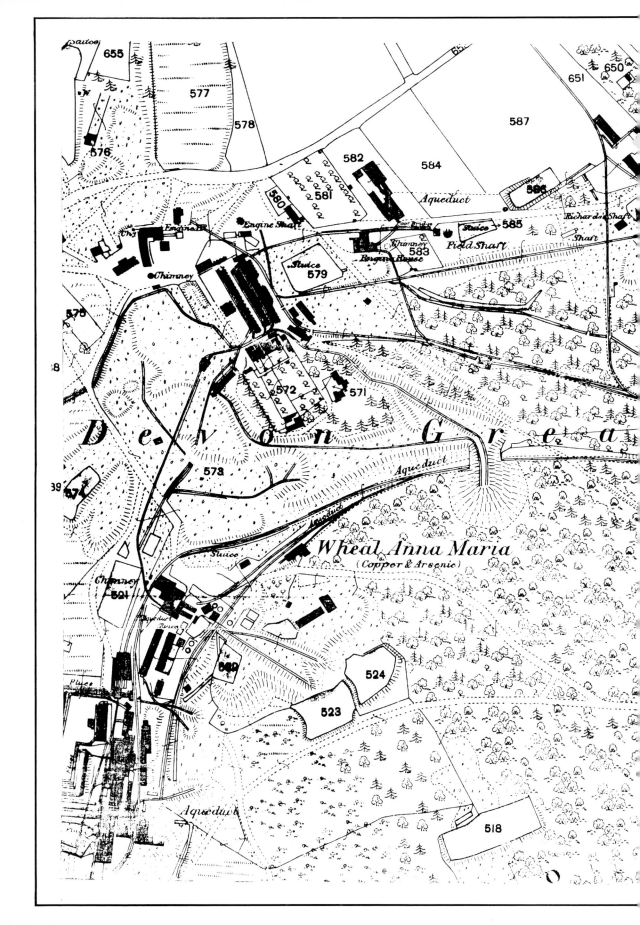

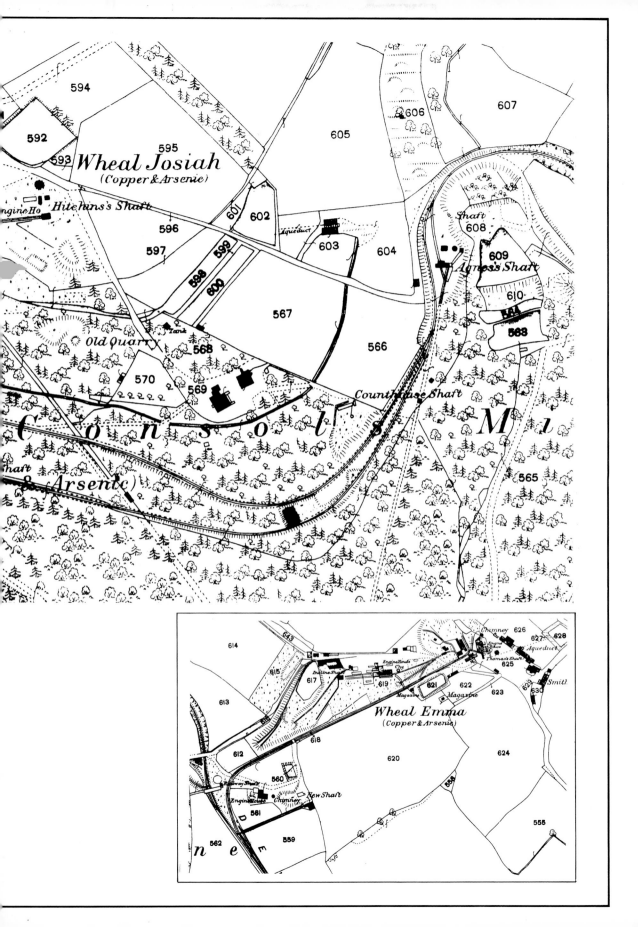

assist in working the new wheel . . . The whole affair is a fine piece of workmanship and does great credit to Messrs Nicholls, Williams and Co., (Tavistock) the engineers responsible for constructing the machinery.

At (the newly opened) Wheal Emma a counting house and also the necessary buildings for the smiths and carpenters were completed. A good road was also made from this mine to the main road of the district.

Wheal Emma was also provided with a steam whim to haul the ore to the surface, and a 40 inch steam pumping engine was also installed. During the same period (1850), a large water wheel 50 feet by 4 feet was also erected at Anna Maria to work the new crusher and stamps there.

The number of people employed and their particular jobs at the mine are given here in a table. They made up a total workforce of 1024 by July 1850. As the mines continued to prosper, so the company increased its investment and its workforce.

The number of persons engaged at these works is, of course, very large. The following is a list of those employed in June and July last. showing the number in each mine and in each department:—

JUNE, 1850.

UNDERGROUND.	Wheal Maria.	Wheal Fanny.	Wheal Josiah.	Wh. Anna Maria.	Wheal Fremcnter.	Wheal Emma.	Wheal Thomas.	Tot.
Tutworkmen	36	71	70	18	4	9	12	220
Tributers	38	50	60	28	—	—	—	176
Trammers, fillers, and landers	9	24	41	8	—	—	—	82
Labourers	—	3	—	3	—	3	2	11
SURFACE.								
Smiths	—	—	—	—	—	—	—	27
Carptrs. & sawyers	—	—	—	—	—	—	—	18
Enginemen	—	—	—	—	—	—	—	11
Masons	—	—	—	—	—	—	—	13
Labourers	—	—	—	—	—	—	—	77
DRESSING PARES.								
Men	9	6	25	4	—	—	—	44
Boys	23	24	63	15	—	—	—	125
Girls	28	46	91	9	—	—	—	174
			Total	978 persons.				
UNDERGROUND.			JULY, 1850.					
Tutworkmen	18	47	48	24	4	9	12	162
Tributers	40	54	72	28	—	—	—	194
Trammers, fillers, and landers	6	24	41	8	—	—	—	82
Labourers	—	3	3	6	—	3	2	17
SURFACE.								
Smiths	—	—	—	—	—	—	—	27
Carptrs. & sawyers	—	—	—	—	—	—	—	18
Enginemen	—	—	—	—	—	—	—	11
Masons	—	—	—	—	—	—	—	10
Labourers	—	—	—	—	—	—	—	82
Stone masons	—	—	—	—	—	—	—	15
DRESSING PARES.								
Men	10	13	25	8	—	—	—	56
Boys	30	33	64	15	—	—	—	142
Girls	36	59	84	20	—	—	—	199
			Total	1015 persons.				

To these, however, have to be added five underground agents, two surface agents, and two storekeepers, making the total number of persons employed in July last 1024.

The railway system at Devon Great Consols was a direct reflection of the productivity and wealth of these mines. Consols claimed the only standard gauge railway line to be entirely owned and worked by a specific mining concern within the West Country. It was built to connect the various parts of the Consols sett with the Tamar and the port of Morwellham. Construction over the $4\frac{1}{2}$ mile route began early in 1857, work being completed in November 1858.

Transport costs by road had been considerable and when the new line opened it was found that expenditure could be cut from 5 shillings a ton by road to 1 shilling a ton by rail.

The railway commenced at Wheal Anna Maria, where large shutes or bins capable of holding up to 200 tons of ore had been constructed. They were built so that the wagons could run beneath/alongside them, enabling the ore to be fed directly into the wagon. A large coal yard was also built at Anna Maria to enable extensive quantities of coal to be stored there instead of being piled on the quays, taking up valuable space.

As far as possible the line followed the level of the land, being planned on a ruling gradient of 1 in 48. Running southward from the mines the line crossed the Tavistock to Gunnislake road and, soon after, negotiated a long S shaped curve passing close to South Bedford and Russel United mines. Thereafter, the line was comparatively straight and led on to the head of the inclined plane marking

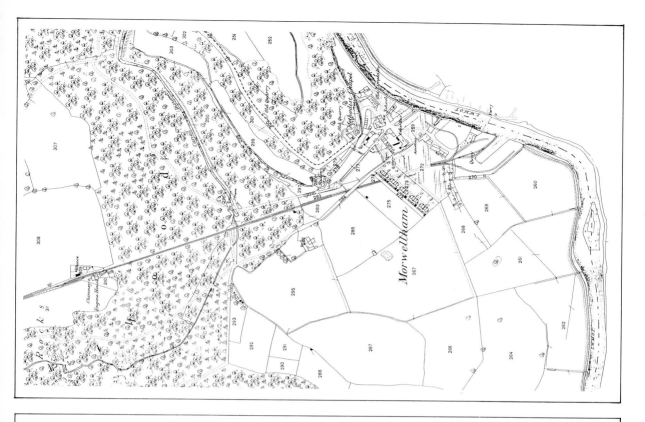

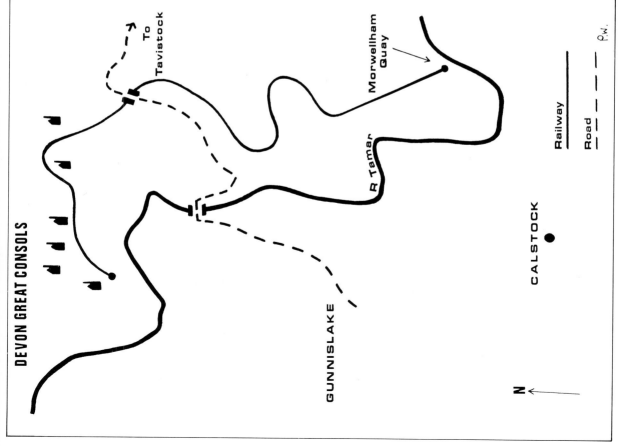

DEVON GREAT CONSOLS

To Tavistock

Morwellham Quay

R Tamar

GUNNISLAKE

CALSTOCK

Railway

Road

P.W.

N

the final half mile to the quays at a gradient of 1 in 3 down the hillside. The inclined plane was worked by a stationary engine, built at Devon Great Consols foundry, this again being an indication of the company's scope. Nine men and two boys were employed at the foundry (July 1860), believed to be the only one to be directly owned by and serving a single mining interest in the tin or copper industry.

The trucks entered and left the quays at Morwellham through a tunnel beneath a row of newly built workers cottages. Special staging was provided for the tracks at the quay. Being raised above the tiled quay itself, the wagons were unloaded directly from their overhead staging. As with the arrangements for loading at the mine, the entire operation was designed to be swift and efficient.

Together with the out-going copper ore, coal and iron ore were imported together, of course, with massive consignments of timber. The great need for timber at Devon Great Consols has already been considered earlier, but it is important to note that a branch off the main line served the saw mills at Wheal Josiah, the timber being brought up the Tamar in raft form.

Development of the dock at Morwellham was part of the overall plan for Devon Great Consols in the late 1850s, along with the railway. The new dock 290 feet long, 60 feet wide, and 16 feet deep was opened in 1859. These works, carried out by the Duke of Bedford at a cost of £5,000, enabled ships of 300 tons to serve the port. That the quays were tiled to prevent wastage of valuable ore has already been noted. Given the financial outlay, the Duke of Bedford levied a toll of 4d per ton on copper ore, 3d per ton on timber and coal, and 2d per ton on iron. In addition, the Duke also required that all goods for himself and his tenants should be carried over the railway at 1 shilling per ton.

It was, of course, vital for all concerned that Morwellham should be developed to cope with the tremendous increase in demand at that time. Prior to the opening of the railway and the development of Morwellham Quay output at the mine was inevitably limited as Gawton Quay, New Quay and Morwellham itself were unable to meet the demand. The combination of railway and newly extended port met the requirement.

The peak of copper production was reached in 1857 with 28,836 tons, by 1872 the figure had fallen to 16,329 tons, and to only 7,481 tons by 1875. Prices, of course, fell with output, adding to problems. Rising costs, deeper and more difficult levels together with the falling prices and cheap foreign imports meant long-term decline, already a factor in most parts of Cornwall. Arsenic production by 1891 had reached 3,500 tons annually.

Arsenic production kept Devon Great Consols in business from the 1880s onward, and it was, eventually, the combination of a fall in arsenic prices and the failure to win necessary contracts for further production which brought about closure. All work ceased in November 1901, but the pumps were kept going. Hopes were fastened upon an upturn in prices and new contracts for arsenic, but in June of the following year the greatest copper mining sett throughout Devon and Cornwall closed.

All machinery and materials were sold during 1903, much of it for scrap. The Duke of Bedford, having found alternative work for the labour force over the winter of 1901/1902, was anxious to restore the entire site to its former woodland condition. The mine buildings, burrows and shafts largely disappeared in the rapid restoration work. Morwellham Quay was left, for the most part, to nature and to silence, until it, too, was the subject of restoration, to its former position as a leading river port of the mid nineteenth century. Morwellham Quay today is an excellent example of initiative and enterprise, recreating, as far as this is ever possible, the atmosphere of a bustling industrial community. Sadly, little, almost nothing remains of the great mining complex which did so much to develop and sustain the port.

The two largest groups of workers employed underground were tut workers and tributers. Tutwork involved sinking the shafts, driving the levels in the mine and the removal of rubble. Before a piece of ground was assigned to a team, the mine agents and the men themselves inspected it and duly costed the work. The men then put a bid for the particular section of ground, with allowances made by the company who paid the expenses and later charged them to the team. An example of these arrangements as set out at Devon Great Consols is given here.

TUTWORK. – The 80 fathom level to drive west of Richards' engine shaft, to be
carried 7 feet high and 4 feet wide, with dead levels by six men, for the
month out.
At £7 per fathom, and 1 shilling in the £1 on the ores taken by:

Richard Osborne, James Sandercock, John Lawry, R. Hooper, J. Sandercock, JNR, William Dunstone.

The account for this work as prepared by the company reads:

DEVON GREAT CONSOLIDATED COPPER MINES
Pay November 1849. Paid January 5 1850

WHEAL JOSIAH

Richard Osborne and partners, driving the 80 fathom level west of Richards' engine shaft – 3 fathoms 3 feet 4 inches at £7 per fathom – £24 17s.9d. Putting in rails – £0 2s.6d – £25 0s.3d.

			£	s	d
Deduct	–	48lbs candles at 8d. per lb	1	12	0
Deduct	–	50lbs powder at 8d. per lb	1	13	4
		Safety Fuse		6	0
		Hilts			3
		Cans		2	6
		Smiths costs		6	10
		Drawing at 10s.	1	15	6
		Doctor and Sick		9	0
		Leaves	16	4	10

Each man, under this particular agreement earned wages of £2 15s 9d. The overall figure of 9 shillings deducted under 'doctor and sick' was the agreed 1s 6d paid by each man in to a fund, set up by the company, to provide medical attention for themselves and their families. Four shillings a week after the first week of illness was then available to those injured at their work.

Tributers were those who worked the ore lodes themselves. They accepted a particular piece of ground on a share basis, working for a month at an agreed contracted rate. The tributers were not then regular wage earning employees always working at a fixed rate. Theirs was a style of work involving both independence and risk. Good judgement in evaluating a piece of ground was therefore required by all parties, miners and employers alike. With a rich lode and the prospect of hard work ahead the tributers could look forward to prosperity; likewise, the mine owners would ensure a quick return, building on their profits, paying, of course, only for the results of the miners' labour. Under the arrangements tributers had to pay for raising the ores to the surface and their preparation for market. A tributers agreement at Devon Great Consols is given here:

DEVONSHIRE GREAT CONSOLIDATED COPPER MINES

TRIBUTE:–   Robert Trethewey's pitch, in the back of the 35 fathom level, west of the eastern engine shaft, so high as the bottom of the 25 level; to extend from Matthews' winze 10 fathoms east; the taken being bound to work and secure their ground as directed by the agents and be subject to the general rules and conditions of mining by six men.
At 7s. 6d in the £1 – Taken by
Samuel Matthews, Henry Stephens,
J. Henwood, John Jewel, William Tyack, A Truscott.

A statement relating to the work similar to that prepared for the tut workers given above was then prepared covering costs, deductions and final balance.

Tutwork and tribute often brought good returns for mining teams on a rich lode, but the work overall took a terrible toll in lives. It was not only an extremely demanding way of life in terms of sheer effort, in many cases it also entailed long-term illness from endless hours in wretched surroundings. Accidents, often fatal, were a common occurrence, but the numerous doctors' reports on miners' health and the findings of the Royal Commissions of Inquiry into these and other mines in

Britain revealed extensive evidence of work-related illness. The Royal Commission of 1864, for example, investigated cases of miners in the Tavistock district. Two such cases are considered here.

The first, relates to a 61 year old miner of the district who had been at work under ground from the age of 9 to 10 years. He was employed at tutwork and tribute. After many years working in conditions where it was said candles would not burn for lack of air, or where they would only burn when carried sideways, he came to Devon Great Consols. Describing conditions there for this man in his middle age, the report said:–

> . . . Came to Wheal Maria (Great Devon) where he worked for 14 years on tribute chiefly, but some tutwork. Worked in very bad air there in the 40 level about 60 or 70 (fathoms) from the shaft. 'It shortened my breath a little but did not lay me up, and I did not think anything of it.' Then went to Wheal Emma for 12 months. The air was bad there in the 20 level, 40 or 50 from draught. He continued to work there for five months. 'I was getting £9 and £10 a month because no one else would work in it, and the agent wanted it cleared away to make a shaft meet the draught.' He then worked for 7 or 8 months on tribute and was then obliged to give up altogether. He has not worked for 2 years and 3 months. (Dated August 1862).

The report continued by stating that three years earlier, after working in these conditions he was taken ill with a bad cough and spat blood for about 3 months intervals. It also stated: 'He has lost flesh very much for 2 years. . . Now complains of weakness sand shortness of breath, sinking in the chest, palpitation of the heart on going up hill.' Further the notes record: 'Habits not very tempered. Says he paid 9d a month for 12 months to the club and 9d for the doctor. He was attended by the mine doctor, but received nothing from the club because he had no hurt.'

Records of another case, that of a 43 year old miner, also on tribute and tutwork, reflects similar experiences:

> First worked at Wheal Franco for 18 months in 24 and 50 levels from surface. Worked in no bad air but plenty of smoke, and there was only one shaft. It was a very hard footway to climb. Then worked at Wheal Friendship, Wheal Betsy, Wheal Marquis and at Devon Great Consols. Worked in bad air in Wheal Friendship on tribute about 20

The house and the mine – a view of Wheal Gorland, near St. Day. This mine was worked successfully for copper in the mid-nineteenth century and, thereafter, for tin, arsenic and tungsten. When finally abandoned in 1911 Wheal Gorland had been employing 61 people, 25 working underground and 36 at the surface. The photograph is dated circa 1905.

Royal Institution of Cornwall

years ago, in the 150 and 170 levels. 'I knew it was bad air by its effects. The candle gives a very dull light so you can hardly touch or look at it without it going out.' Felt ill effects from it.

This man went on to work in Australia before returning to Cornwall, then Devon. He had begun work underground at the age of 14, but by August 1862 had been unable to work for 15 months. Headache, aching legs, palpitations of the heart, cough and general weakness were noted as his particular problem.

'The Report of the Commissioners Appointed to Inquire into the Condition of All Mines in Great Britain', 1864, offered extensive detail on the state of miners' health. Thomas B Peacock, Physician to St Thomas' Hospital, and to the Hospital for Disease of the Chest, presented the medical report. His work was carried out largely amongst the miners of West Cornwall, but the findings were applicable to all districts of West Devon and Cornwall. The research was completed during July and August 1862.

Beginning with general appearance, Thomas Peacock wrote:

> In examining, even casually, a large number of miners, it is impossible not to be struck with the peculiarly delicate appearance of many of them, and especially of the older men and of the boys and young men who have worked underground only for a short time. Instead of having the bright and clear complexions of the young people employed at the surface, those who labour in the mines have a very pale, sallow appearance . . . Comparatively few men are found at work who have much passed the middle period of life, and still fewer who under such circumstances appear and report themselves to be in good health.

On the evidence of a return covering the whole of Cornwall and West Devon, The Royal Commission on Mines calculated the average age of employment underground at 28.91 years. Prosper United Mine at Marazion had a high average of 41.46 years, whilst Wheal Seton at Pool, between Camborne and Redruth, gave an average age of 22.45 years. Deep mining was young men's work, the most productive years being between the ages of 20 and 40, thereafter, the ability to continue work underground fell away significantly.

Respiratory disease was the greatest killer, but dyspeptic and rheumatic complaints were also significant, the former being, to a certain extent, attributable to diet. The miner's traditional meal, the pasty, was described in Thomas Peacock's medical report as consisting of "a paste of flour, water and suet, with a small quantity of meat – fresh meat or port, and potatoes and other vegetables. It is both an innutritous and indigestible article of food and may in some degree explain the frequency with which miners suffer from dyspeptic conditions".

The Reverend John Pretyman Berkeley, vicar of St Cleer, near Liskeard, described Cornish pasties as 'complete engines for the destruction of health, especially in the case of the miner.' On returning home from work, the miner in the Liskeard district would have a meal of broth made of a lump of fat and some vegetables. It was stated that miner's wives rarely bought more than seven pounds of meat a week, and that this amount would be considered 'a large supply' for a man and wife with three or four children.

Further west, at Camborne, Dr Peacock's investigations into miner's families and their personal history included the following statement on a man examined in July 1862 and having been employed locally at East Wheal Crofty and Dolcoath mines:

> When working he states that he has earned from £3 10s to £5 per month and he has a wife and three children to support. He rises at about 4.30 am and gets underground by 6, having to get his breakfast and walk about a mile. He works underground for eight hours. His breakfast consists of a cup of tea and bread and butter; he takes also some water and bread and butter underground. When he returns at 2pm he gets his dinner which consists of a mutton chop, soup and vegetables. He seldom has any beer with it; he thinks he may take about 1/2 lb of cooked meat a day and a pint of beer, never any spirit unless he is not well.

This man was described as having a 'tolerable appetite' but complained that his food lay 'heavy in his stomach.' He was diagnosed as having miner's asthma, disorder of the digestive organs, hepatic symptoms and diarrhoea. By comparison with certain others interviewed this man enjoyed a reasonable diet, although some others made more mention of vegetables and eggs.

Direct comparisons were made between miners and farmworkers regarding diet and health. Mr.

Philip Vincent, a surgeon to several mines in the Camborne district was asked by the Commission to comment on these two different ways of life. In answer to the question: 'Who lives best; the miner or the agriculturalist?' Vincent replied:

> The miner is rather improvident about it; it is rather a feast and a fast with him. One day he will have his beef-steaks or his good living, and the next day he will have his porridge, and they live upon broth, as they call it, for some days afterwards, and only throw in a bone or bit of pork to make the porridge. The agriculturalist generally gets his regular allowance from the farmer, and so it is regulated much better than it is with the miner.

Whilst it was agreed generally that miners ate more meat, the agricultural population across the county was considered to be better fed and healthier. This was largely a recognition of the fact that the farming community had more immediate means to a balanced diet, not that they ate in greater quantities.

The rheumatic complaints came from the constant exposure to damp and wet, and the difficulty of drying working clothes, and, not least, to the damp Cornish climate and conditions at home.

Damp and the obvious extremes of temperature encouraged respiratory problems. Peacock's report stated that a large proportion of the cases of asthma, bronchitis and consumption began with symptoms of cold. The combination of high temperatures into the upper 80s and 90s, sometimes higher, the intensely physical nature of the work, the climb to and from their work place and the effects of poor ventilation, confined space and the inevitable dust, made it almost impossible not to develop respiratory difficulties.

When working in extreme heat, miners told the Royal Commission that they frequently stood or bathed in cold water to cool themselves; in every case, it was stated that they could only work for very short periods at a time, because of rapid exhaustion. The fact that in many parts of the mines, there was insufficient air to enable the candles to burn freely illustrates the problem of ventilation. Many miners spoke of the need to turn their candles on edge, or almost invert them, to get any light at all..

Evidence from John Sampson, a miner from the Caradon district, near Liskeard, provided valuable details of this destructive working environment. Questioned on its effects, Sampson said the confined space and bad air made him feel 'weak, sleepy and stupid, and I almost always had a headache; a sick headache.' The first symptoms were splitting headache and fatigue of the limbs, complaints that were hardly surprising in view of the working place, and the fact that the men were employed in such conditions for three months:

> The greater part of the time, the candle would burn scarcely at all, and at the latter end when we were close upon holing, the candle would go out more than 50 times a day and we had to keep lighting it with a match, and to keep it almost flat to make it burn at all, and to keep picking it with a pin. We could not stand longer than shooting two holes, and had then to go away or our head would be splitting.

It was explained that the men could only work a six hour day under such circumstances and that the work could only be carried on for a period of an hour without a break and movement elsewhere to breathe better air.

Copper mines also tended to be very deep, 200 fathoms being quite common, which meant that the climb at the end of an eight hour shift would take on average over 40 minutes; the descent, thirty. In the deeper mines to 300 fathoms and more, the climb could take more than an hour. The combination of regular strenuous exercise such as this with the extreme variation of temperature, as stated, ranging from the 80s at least, to perhaps sub-zero surface condition, or the frequent wet and windy weather of a winter's night, would, given time, undoubtedly destroy even the strongest of men. Many of the mines were also in isolated areas involving a walk, to and from work, often of more than a mile or so.

Due care and attention in the provision of dries, or changing houses, also dining areas for surface workers, formed one of the recommendations of the Royal Commission into the Mines, 1862. South Caradon and Dolcoath mines, for example, offered the workforce far superior facilities than most others.

At South Caradon the miner's 'dry' accommodated 400 men. Their working clothes were dried for them, ready for their next shift, whilst their 'walking clothes' could be likewise dried by the time they finished their work should they have been damp or wet when walking from home. Washing facilities were also made available.

A group scene of miners at the 278 fathom level at Levant Mine on the cliffs near Pendeen, West Cornwall, July 1894. The photograph shows miners of all ages, the nature of their work and its effects upon them not being too apparent here, other than in facial expressions
Royal Institution of Cornwall

Bal-maidens and other surface workers pause for the camera at Dolcoath's New East Shaft. Over 1300 people were employed at Dolcoath in the early 1890s when Dolcoath was still rich in tin. The bal-maidens here would receive between 1 shilling and 1 shilling and 2d per day for what was obviously hard relentless labour.
Royal Institution of Cornwall

Bal-maidens, believed to be at Dolcoath, Cornwall's deepest mine, in 1893. The women are working in the tin washing sheds, the circular structures seen in this photograph being the buddles where the tin went through part of the process of washing and grading. Because of their distinctive shape these buddles can often be seen at abandoned mining setts across the county, particularly at Botallack Mine.

Cornish Studies Library

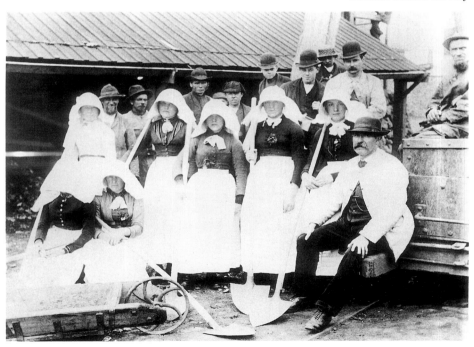

This view shows yet another posed composition with the women in their distinctive bonnet head-dress, aprons and holding the famous Cornish shovels. Whilst always interesting in showing the actual people, the women are clearly dressed in their best for the camera, thus it is difficult to appreciate the hard physical labour required of them.

Cornish Studies Library

Dolcoath prided itself regarding amenities for its workforce, as the Royal Commission described:

This is the largest tin mine in Cornwall and is very well provided with suitable accommodation for the comforts of the people.

The changing house is about 25 fathoms from the man engine (machinery for raising and lowering men in the mine and usually a feature of the largest, most profitable concerns) shaft. It is 80 feet long by 22 feet wide and 20 feet high. It has 11 windows, glazed and capable of being opened. There is also a large ventilator in the roof formed by raising a portion 17 feet in length about 6 or 8 inches. This is always open. A gallery runs around three sides. It has a wooden floor. It is warmed by a fire and tube 41 feet long. Around the ground floor are the men's lockers, each being 2 feet 2 inches long, 1 foot 10 inches wide and 1 foot 6 inches deep. Before the man engine was employed, the footway shaft opened into this changing house. The number of men changing here is about 350. These are divided into several corps, some commencing at 6 am, others at 7; others again at 2 pm and the night corps at 10pm, so that the number changing at any one time will rarely be more than 70 or 80.

The dressing floors are very large, giving employment to 570 persons. Of this number, 260 are girls. The operations are carried on in large yards, enclosed and roofed in.

There are four houses set apart for the dressers to dine in. For each house a woman is hired whose duty it is to keep it clean, have kettles boiling and everything ready for those employed when they leave work at 10 and 12 o'clock for refreshment.

These were obviously the best of conditions; there were far less inspired examples in many of the smaller mines where men might consider themselves fortunate to get any clothing dried in the engine houses themselves, not as a right, but as an unofficial practice.

Large numbers of women and girls were employed at the surface workings of the tin and copper mines. The bal-maidens, as they were known, performed the tasks linked to the processing of the ore at the surface. Their work was described in an article for the *Mining Journal* in 1858, but the writer, George Henwood, gave them a somewhat bad press, choosing characteristically for that period, a decidedly moralistic tone, far outweighing the physical and medical dimensions involved:

In tin mines these girls attend to the frames which is comparatively light and clean work, but continual exposure to wet is unfit for females, whilst the constant association with the men and boys is highly improper. These poor girls remain from the early age mentioned until they either get married to some of the miners or die of consumption, which carries off hundreds annually.

The hard work is not the greatest calamity of which we complain, that is a mere physical evil. What we most deplore is that when called to take upon themselves the duties of wife and mother they are entirely unfit for them. How can the moral standards of society amongst the lower orders be raised by mothers and sisters with such education and example? It is utterly hopeless. Taken from their hearth at such an early age and kept at work for ten hours a day, they have little opportunity and less inclination to attend to the matronly duties so necessary for their future and well being. Their being associated in such numbers and before men, a spirit or rivalry in dress is soon engendered and every attention – all their thoughts and earnings – are devoted to the methods of making themselves attractive.

To see the bal-maidens on a Sunday when fully dressed would astonish a stranger; whilst at their work the pendant earrings and the showy bead necklaces excite the pity, as well as the surprise of the thoughtful. All desire to save a few shillings for later life is discarded and nothing but display is thought of.

Machinery is rapidly effecting a change and we hail every improvement in that department as a real blessing to miners; but where it dispenses with female labour, in such situation, we rejoice in it as a grand and effective effort towards the domestic comfort of thousands, and as a help towards the elevation of the social position of mankind generally.

A poor standard of housing amongst the mining communities was widely regarded as an important factor influencing health in general. Evidence from all the mining districts reflected this. Thomas Peacock reported on Wendron, Near Helston and St Just in August 1862:

At Wendron they consist of low buildings with thatched roofs, containing two rooms. In one which I visited there were three beds in a small room upstairs, without any window which permitted of being opened. In this room there was a father who was ill and a wife with a little baby in one bed, a married daughter with a baby in the second bed, and the rest of the family consisted of the son-in-law, a daughter of about 16, and two sons of 14 and 12. In none of these cottages was there any drainage or privies.

The cottages in the St Just district were also generally most defective. They were small, low and thatched; contained only two rooms for large families, and the little windows provided in the sleeping rooms would rarely open. The floors were of concrete, and there was no under drainage and rarely any privy, the whole refuse being thrown out on a dirt heap in front of the door, or into a pool of dirty, green water through which it was often necessary to pick the way to reach the door. This district is elevated and perfectly open to the sea and should be most healthy, but from the neglect of all attention to sanitary regulations, it was suffering from typhoid fever and I was informed that the disease had been prevailing extensively and fatally for several months.

Peacock did not, however, consider that bad housing offered any particular explanation for the poor health of the miners, arguing that their families would have been far more influenced by this.

All sections of the working community, in particular, were very much affected by consumption and the respiratory diseases generally. This was highlighted by Dr Charles Barham, Senior Physician to Truro Infirmary. Respiratory disease produced the highest sickness and death rates of all categories listed in Barham's detailed inquiry into the conditions at Truro in the late 1830s. Richard Couch, a mine surgeon in West Cornwall published valuable comparative material in his 'Statistical Investigations into the Mortality of Miners'. In the Marazion district the average death rate from consumption amongst miners was 64.49 per cent, whilst amongst non miners it was 30.92 per cent, the survey taking place over the period 1838-1856. In the St Just district at the mid century the death rate from consumption amongst miners was 49.66 per cent and 28.39 per cent for those otherwise employed. Mining served to intensify the serious existing problem of disease within the community. Richard Sleman, a surgeon at Tavistock, on the far eastern edge of the mining districts, took a different view from Thomas Peacock. He saw a direct link between the miners' poor health and the hopeless housing common to most of them. Asked by the Mines' Commission to state the main medical problem experienced by the miners, Sleman answered with a comparison of two local districts, Mary Tavy and Bere Alston:

At Mary Tavy, in consequence of the habitations of the miners being adequate to the population we do not get much fever. If you go to Bere Alston, where the number of houses is just the same, but where the population is 2,000 as against 500, you get more fever and more disease generally, and so at Gunnislake. I believe that the disease depends more on the habitation of the miner than anything else.

Sleman continued by stating that miners' disease – respiratory complaints, asthma, bronchitis and consumption – was made much worse by the poor home environment:

You have that, superadded to the other drawbacks upon him; first of all he has irregular hours, then when he gets home he has a miserable place to sleep in; he may be sleeping in the same room as that in which his wife is washing in the same day . . . I draw the inference that the dwellings have a good deal to do with the matter from the fact that at the deepest mine in our neighbourhood, Wheal Friendship, the miners disease is not prevalent, and the cottages are not so filled.

Wheal Friendship was generally considered to offer superior conditions for its workforce. Although deep at 240 fathoms, it was a well ventilated mine; there were changing houses for the men, their clothes being dried for them before going underground, and where their wet clothes, on their arrival at the mine, could be dried by the time they finished work, to return home. Facilities like these obviously helped to promote better health, and taken together with the absence of overcrowding in the home, worked directly in the miner's favour. Improved standards of health depended ultimately upon both reasonable working conditions and a tolerable home environment, the latter being particularly desirable in view of the arduous nature of mining as a way of life.

William Gard, manager of East Gunnislake, South Bedford and Old Gunnislake Mines also regarded housing as a major factor in damaging the miner's health. He was quite firm in his view:

I believe that there is nothing which tends so much to the deterioration of the miners'

Glebe Stamps with New Wendron Consols engine house seen on the skyline. The thatched cottage here and the family group offer a scene close in description and character to that of the Royal Commission's findings of 1864, which focussed on miners' housing. This fascinating photograph is dated circa 1880, offering us an excellent record of the mining community in the Helston district.

Royal Institution of Cornwall

Miners cottages provided for those at work in the Devon Great Consols sett. Such accommodation, purpose built and part of a number of such houses built in the district, gave standards way above that of most mining communities in West Devon and Cornwall. It was the exception rather than the rule, these cottages being provided by the Duke of Bedford.

Royal Institution of Cornwall

health as the state in which all these little dirty villages are found.

As chairman of the local health committee, Gard attempted to introduce improvements at Gunnislake. He gave the Royal Commission of 1864 the following statement illustrating the difficulties in actually implementing essential improvements:

I was chairman of the local committee for two years and took a lot of interest in trying to have the Sanitary Act carried out, but was beaten by the owners of cottages; they found out that I was *making them drain*. In the committee I had farmers for my team; they were very difficult to drive at first, but at last I got them to work the Act, and when owners found that they were compelled to drain and remove pigsties, and put up water closets, those who owned these miners' cottages immediately set to work and we were all turned out together. There were two medical men, Dr Sellers and Mr Wood. We were all sacked at once, and a set of men were put in purposely not to carry the Act out.

Hardship and endurance on the part of the miner and his family was part of the way of life above, and below, ground. Even the official statistics presented the situation in a better light than actual experience proved. Richard Couch, mine surgeon, questioned the accuracy of the registry of death. Detailed research on his part, and close familiarity with the miners' circumstances led him to write the following:

It may be stated as a fact, that there is a very great difference between the average ages of the miners, as recorded in the registry of death, and those who consult you for disease, or whom you have to attend for accident. There is a source of error, therefore, somewhere. To ascertain the cause of so great a disparity, I applied to several gentlemen of St Just and neighbourhood, who had influence over the mines, and by them I have been supplied with returns of the names and ages of all the men employed, together with the length of time they have been engaged in mining. These valuable returns will enable a comparison to be instituted between the ages of those actually engaged in work and their ages at death. The average ages of miners, according to the registry of death, is from 1837 to 1856:

Year	Average age	Year	Average age	Year	Average age	Year	Average age
1837	49.6	1842	45.10	1847	53.0	1852	42.0
1838	45.5	1843	52.2	1848	52.2	1853	46.2
1839	47.3	1844	48.4	1849	49.4	1854	47.6
1840	44.0	1845	42.7	1850	44.9	1855	44.7
1841	50.0	1846	45.5	1851	49.1	1856	41.6

The maximum average for any year was in 1847, when it rose to 53 years of age; and the minimum average was 1852, when it sunk to 42 years of age; and the average of the whole period of twenty years is 47, a longevity which is considerably above the age of the working miner. I have selected three for special reference in three distant localities, – Balleswidden, Levant and Ding Dong. In estimating the age of the working miner, I have been as liberal to the class as consistently with truth it was possible to be. All are considered as miners who are working underground, or who have ever done so, provided they are at present employed on the mine; and in the class I have placed such men as are employed in timber-work below the surface. This will of course make the result less unfavourable than if reference were made only to such as are employed underground as miners, or who have been employed at the surface for one year. The seed of disease sown under ground frequently compels a man to seek occupation at the surface; and there he may linger on for years, and finally dying of the 'miners' disease,' ought to be considered a victim to mining operations. I have taken into consideration every circumstance likely favourably to influence the result.

In Balleswidden, there are three hundred and three men and boys employed in what may be called mining operations, and the average age of all is 29 years and 4 months. But if we omit from the calculation the timber-men, and such as only go below occasionally, the average age sinks to 26 years and 9 months for the working miner. The youngest miner engaged below the surface is 11 years of age; the oldest is 74 years of age, but he is too feeble for his employment, and is employed only in the shallow levels. The ages at which the greatest number are employed ranges from 11 to 25 years of age.

In Levant Mine, where there are two hundred and six men and boys who are now or were formerly engaged as miners, the average age is 28 years and 10 months; but the average age of such as would be considered miners is 27 years and 4 months, the greatest number fluctuating between 10 and 25 years of age. The two youngest are 10 years of age, and the two oldest are 71 and 74 years of age; the one aged 71 years is still employed underground, and the other aged 74 years, has been employed at the surface for some years. In Ding Dong, there are two hundred and six men and boys employed, and the average age of all is 26 years and 1 month; but if we take only such men as are actually engaged below, the age sinks to 24 years: the two youngest are 8 years of age, much too young, and the oldest, 74 years of age, who is employed as dry-man at the surface. The ages of the greatest number employed fluctuates between the ages of 8 and 20 years.

In the three mines here examined, which may be fairly taken as specimens of mines in general, and were not selected for any special purpose, it will be observed that the ages of working miners are less than those recorded in the registry of death. The difference is so very great that a little further examination is required. The annexed table will show not only the average age, but the ages at which there is most employment:

Table showing ages of employment:–

Names of Mines	8to15	-20	-25	-30	-35	-40	-45	-50	-55	-60	-65	-70	-75	Ave age
Balleswidden	41	44	47	28	24	25	15	14	16	6	2	1	1	29.4
Levant	29	45	37	16	15	12	18	15	13	3	0	0	2	28.1
Ding Dong	61	52	17	17	9	18	10	9	7	10	3	0	1	26.1

From this table it appears that more men are employed between 15 and 20 years of age than at any other period; and that, next in order, more are employed between 8 and 15 years of age: but as the numbers so closely aproximate, it is very probable that in some districts more may be employed below 15 years of age than any other similar period. Between the ages of 10 and 20 years, therefore, seems to be the age of greatest employment: from these ages there is a gradual decrease as years roll on; but between 40 and 55 years of age, there is a fluctuation of a few up and down. The early deaths arising from accident, therefore, is fully explained. The doctrines of probabilities being fully equal to explain everything respecting it. This point being ascertained, it cannot be very difficult to explain the difference between the average age of the miner, as indicated by the registry of death, and that indicated by the men actually engaged in the mine. Accidents are numerous, disease is powerful in preventing a miner from continuing his employment. Some men fail sooner than others; but nearly all are obliged, as they advance in age, to seek to perform the lighter and more healthy part of their duties at the surface, leaving the more laborious and unhealthy to the younger men: many are incapacitated altogether. Some, from explosions, lose the sight of both eyes, others may lose a hand, and occasionally a foot. Thoracic diseases also exert their influence in making a man retire altogether from his work; and thus, compelling them to depend either on the precarious club, or to fall at once with their families on the Union. In this state they may lie up for years without occupation, and yet, when they die, become registered as miners. In some cases I have known dependant on charity for twenty years, without having been occupied in a mine for a single hour; but still in death they are placed in the registry as miners. To this there can be no objection; but still it is necessary to bear it in mind, when such differences are observed between two such authentic sources of information as the registry of death and register of the mine. The average age of the miner, according to the registry of death, is 47 years, – according to the returns from the mines, is 37 years; but his active life, supposing it to commence at 10 years of age, terminates in eighteen years, at the early age of 28 years, when in most other occupations he would be in the prime of manhood and of vigour.

EAST WHEAL ROSE DISASTER

Together with its extensive copper deposits, Cornwall was well known, perhaps best known, for its tin mining. There were also notable iron and lead workings, concentrated mainly in mid-county, but in all of these concerns, large or small, accidents were a common occurrence. Some were obviously more serious than others, but injury and, inevitably, loss of life, were clearly part of mining experience. Large scale disasters, however, were comparatively rare being much more a feature of the collieries than of metalliferous mining.

Cornwall's worst mining disaster was visited upon East Wheal Rose, a prosperous lead mining sett in the parish of Newlyn East. Thirty-nine men and boys died there in the early afternoon of 9 July 1846. Death came suddenly and swiftly; horribly, and in terrible irony. It came, not from the more likely sources of danger underground but from the skies. They died from drowning when a freak thunderstorm unleashed its torrents of water onto the immediate vicinity of the mine, flooding the workings. Two miles south-west, the village of Zelah had no rain at all; Mitchell, a village less than two miles to the south-east, experienced only slight rainfall.

At the time of the disaster East Wheal Rose was an important concern employing 1,266 men, women and children. The mine workings were situated on low ground forming a basin or vale, of sorts, and surrounded almost on all sides by highground, with only what is now the narrow Lappa Valley, running northward, natural drainage was limited. The disaster was reported at length in the Cornish press, and was featured in the *Mining Journal*. According to the *Royal Cornwall Gazette* there were unmistakable signs of abnormal weather by midday:

> Between twelve and one o'clock, immense masses of black clouds overhung all the hills surrounding East Wheal Rose, and extended as far as the eye could see. A terrible thunder-storm commenced; the lightning was very vivid; the rolling of the thunder, loud. About one o'clock the rain poured down in such a lashing torrent, as eye-witnesses stated, they never before saw in England . . . The consequence was that in an incredibly short space of time large streams of water poured down the hills surrounding East Wheal Rose with impetuous force, and uniting at the bottom, formed almost 'a perfect sea of water' which rushed on from south to north in the direction of the valley and directly over the area of the sett.

The mine workings ran parallel with the small river running down through the valley and the main shafts were, therefore, directly in the path of the water wall. These shafts running northward were ten in number, the nearest, Oxnams and Davey's shafts, flooding first, and with the combined effect of the water pouring down the line of shafts, survivors told of a mighty rush of wind throughout the mine, extinguishing their candles. Thus the perils of darkness and complete confusion were added to the nightmare of innundation. In the attempt to convey the power and impact of the flood, reports described the massive sections of timber used at the mine as being broken and washed considerable distances away southward to a locality known as Metha Bridge. A substantial new road bridge, part of a new road westward to Zelah, was destroyed by the force of the flood, and, afterwards, the road itself was said to be up to two feet deep in mud.

No blame was attributed to the management of the mine. Captain Middleton, in charge of the workings, gave orders prior to the flood, and at the time it first began to rain, that men at the surface should clear the leats to ensure adequate drainage. The leats were considered sufficient to carry any 'normal' amount of water experienced in the wettest of winters. Men were also put to work storing timbers and barrows and, specifically, building protective collars of earth and stone around the heads of the shafts to keep back the water. These precautions were of no avail, however, given the severity of the flood waters, and in the darkness and terror below ground the men did what they could to save themselves. All the steam engines were set to work bringing the men to the surface as fast as possible. Over 200 miners were below ground at the time, working to a maximum depth of 100 fathoms. The main work, however, was carried out at the 50 fathom level, this one extending for over a mile. It was fortunate that the men were changing shifts at the time of the flooding so that many were near the shafts, but not all. At the inquest, held in the count house, the following day, Samuel Bastion was one miner called to give evidence:

> I am a miner and worked in East Wheal Rose; I was at work in the south part of the mine, at Turner's shaft, about one o'clock yesterday. We had candles, and in that part

Chacewater, between Redruth and Truro, as photographed, circa 1905. This view, westward, along Fore Street looked in the direction of the nearby mining setts of Great Wheal Busy and Killifreth, two of the mines so closely linked with this community, into the early decades of this century.

Royal Institution of Cornwall

of the mine where I was working they were all blown out by a rush of air, which alarmed us, and we proceeded to grass as soon as we could. As soon as we got to the surface, I found that the water was rushing into different parts of the mine, but more particularly into Magor's shaft. the miners were then escaping by the different footways in the best way they could. I afterwards went down to Mitchell's sump shaft, and tried to turn the water away from going into the manhole. I succeeded in diverting it from the manhole and eighteen men came up afterwards. I went down within six feet of the forty fathom level, and had account that there were more men down in the plot, but no more came up after that party of eighteen. I came up again, put on a dry suit of clothes and went over and put a dam to keep the water back. We went to work to search for the bodies about six o'clock on Friday morning at Gower's shaft in the fifty fathom level, and between nine and ten, we found the body of Samuel Wherry; James Coade was in another part of the same plot, and they were both quite dead. We could not find the way down for some time, not knowing the road, some tributers having been working there. The water had been to the back of the level where these men were drowned.

The *Royal Cornwall Gazette* gathered its information from the survivors, portraying a scene of extreme confusion and terror:

As the kibbles (buckets for raising the ore) descended in Gower's shaft the drowning men caught hold of them and were drawn up in clusters, as many as could hold on. The men also frequently caught hold of the chains and were drawn up; one man, it was stated, coming up with merely a finger or two hitched in the chain. At one time, six men were drawn up holding on by the kibble; and when it again descended to the fifty fathom level a man named Harris, and two boys, jumped in, but the water was coming down so forcibly that, when they were raised about six fathoms above the fifty, the two boys were washed out. Several men hanging by the kibbles are said to have been so exhausted that they loosened their hold, and fell down the shafts. In Mitchell's whim shaft some of the miners climbed the open shaft by holding on to the casing, the water rising close to their heels as they ascended. Others saved themselves by climbing fathoms against the force of the water streaming down on them.

Forty-two men were known to be missing by the evening, but early on the Friday morning four of these were found alive in the fifty fathom level. Thirty-eight men and boys died at East Wheal Rose; one man died at the neighbouring North Wheal Rose also flooded at the same time.

The local community braced itself to meet the consequences. Many of those killed were married with children and an appeal was organised on behalf of those affected. *The Mining Journal* took the opportunity to press for greater safety legislation and called for assistance for those distressed by such calamities.

The Journal challenged those it called, 'the miners' friends', to arouse themselves, in view of what had happened, 'to impress upon them the moral duty of that large body of wealthy and influential individuals who derive fortunes from the exertions of the working miner', to act accordingly. The Bishop of Exeter and the local clergy contributed and collected for the relief fund recognising the scale of the tragedy and the suffering and loss experienced by the local community. *The Cornish Banner; A Religious, Literary and Historical Register for the West of England*, however, could not let the events pass without offering its particular contribution; one of very different substance and character:

> Among so large a number of persons were employed at East Wheal Rose – 1260 – there were many of a very wicked and abandoned character; and, by many persons on the spot, the visitation is looked upon in the light of a judgement . . . We trust that a salutary and lasting impression has been produced upon the minds of many persons in the neighbourhood . . .

Not being party to that special insight and awareness of *The Cornish Banner*, the coroner returned verdicts of 'accidental death' on the men and boys of East Wheal Rose.

As *The Mining Journal* noted, 'the exertions of the working miner' were instrumental in making the fortunes of landowners and larger shareholders in the mines. Devon Great Consols and Consolidated Mines at Gwennap were more than proof of this. The industry overall also gave rise to, and sustained, all manner of related trades and occupations, supplying and serving it. Transport – principally railways, shipping and harbour development – foundries, builder's merchants, retail suppliers etc, all benefitted from prosperity in the mines. To this end, the county maintained a large population that increased significantly over the period 1800 to the 1860s, thereafter falling away, with the rapid decline of copper mining and the onset of enforced emigration.

The water-carrier going about his business in Church Street, St. Day, on 19th January, 1928. Mrs Mary Ann Hensley is seen here passing her bucket to 'Blind David.' This formerly rich and populous mining community presented a very different image of Cornwall in the 1920s to that offered by the two railway companies in tourist development. *Royal Institution of Cornwall*

One of George Henwood's frequent contributions to *The Mining Journal* in the late 1850s included this piece on Chacewater as a typical mining community. Henwood conveys the character and atmosphere of the village in the familiar, unsparing style of much mid nineteenth century writing.

This village appears to be a colony of miners who have worked in mines in various parts of the world. Scarcely a family is to be found one member at least of whom has not been out either to Mexico, California, Brazil, New Zealand, Australia, Africa, Spain, or some mining district of less account; in many instances their wives have accompanied them. The Portuguese and Spanish is well and very generally spoken by them when conversing on the subject of their foreign experience. It is not only amusing but highly instructive to listen to the details of their trials by field and flood. From these it is to be gathered that the first who went out to Cuba to work the copper mines suffered far greater loss by death than later emigrants to that country – partly owing to the inexperience of those early visitors, and partly to the carelessness of the miners themselves. Many have returned a second time, and some remained in the country for fifteen years and upwards. Nearly all secured a little competency, to enable them to get into some way of business, a public-house or beer-shop being the principal and favourite speculation. Some few have realised sufficient to maintain themselves in a state of independence. Nearly all the officers on the foreign mines are Cornishmen, and, from the representations of the miners, appear to be admirably conducted and carefully wrought.

In close proximity to Chacewater some mines of great celebrity have been worked, including Scorrier, North Downs, Wheal Rose, Treskerby, Hallenbeagle, Great Wheal Busy, Wheal Seymour, Wheal Daniel, Creegbrawse, the United Mines, St.Day United, Consols, & C., returning many hundreds of thousands of pounds profit, and employing a very great population. The entire village, and much of the neighbourhood, is the property of the Earl of Falmouth. When the mines were in their palmy days Chacewater was a place of considerable importance as a mining village; a capital market-house was built for the convenience of the people, but has since been almost deserted. As the mines became abandoned Chacewater fell in to decay and poverty. By the spirited endeavours of a few individuals the Great Wheal Busy has been set to work, where upwards of 700 people are employed – a great advantage and blessing to the locality. Although this great undertaking has not yet made profitable returns to the adventurers, its promising appearance and satisfactory progress has stimulated adventure, and many mines have been, or are about to be, put to work by powerful companies. Within a radius of four miles of the place many millions of pounds worth of copper and tin ores have been raised and sold.

The village, as a consequence of the resumption of the mines, is reassuming its former *status*. Several good substantial shops have been occupied by a superior class of tradesmen; and two or three good inns are to be found, mine hosts of which do all in their power for the comfort of their guests. Other shops are being erected, but the stringent clauses of Lord Falmouth's leases (all the property is built on leases of three lives) militates against the building a superior class of houses. The places of worship are well and regularly attended, and the ministers much respected. A cricket club, and freemasons' lodge of no mean pretensions, have been established; indeed, the place presents all the elements and appearances of a thriving mining village. Long may it continue, and be emulated.

The town, too, has all the peculiarities belonging to country places. Everybody knows everybody's business better than their own, and act accordingly; this will cure itself as the population increases and business becomes more active, when they will have "other fish to fry" than talking scandal. Here, too, may be found the sharp, shrewd, witty, and persevering tradesman, with a joke and a kind greeting to all he comes in communication with. Here too is the half-witted butt; and the intelligent, kind, and respected doctor, known to all and knowing all, "breed, seed, and generation." Here too, is the connection in business, engendered by family marriages and relationship, that almost prevents the success of any stranger endeavouring to establish a trade; this

Left: Working mines were never 'environmentally friendly' as shown here in this view of Tresavean Mine at Lanner, near Redruth. The well-known tin mine closed down in 1928, one of a small number of mines that had sustained the industry and the ailing economy of the Camborne-Redruth district, in the early part of this century.

Royal Institution of Cornwall

Below: Two views of Killifreth engine house, near Chacewater, October 1991. These two – interior and exterior – views reflect the way in which Cornwall's mining heritage is, here, carefully preserved, emphasising the appeal of the past in tourism today. *Author*

however, will be remedied by the extension of commerce, necessarily following the exertions at present being made to prosecute the Chacewater mines.

The markets are amply and cheaply supplied, and the people well employed, contented, hospitable, and well conducted. We should like to see many villages equally prosperous and promising as the village of Chacewater, the centre of a great mining district. Though her sons may be occasionally deported to work foreign mines, they frequently return to their homes laden with wealth, improved by mixture in superior society, and the experience travel always engenders, the beneficial effects of which cannot fail being imparted to all with whom they are connected, having, as experience shows, an elevating, self-respect creating tendency, as well as a finer appreciation of the benefits by which they are surrounded, and is an inducement to thankfulness to Him by whom all these blessings have been accorded.

CORNWALL'S POPULATION – 1801 - 1901
1801 - 192,281
1831 - 301,306
1861 - 369,390
1881 - 330,686
1901 - 322,320

For all their phenomenal success, the mines were inevitably finite undertakings. As the working went deeper so the work became more complicated and costly; the equality of the ore declined and prices fell making many projects unprofitable. Foreign competition, in the form of bulk imports of high grade ore, delivered the final blow to copper mining, just as it was to do to tin at a later date. With little or no alternative work, large sections of the mining community looked to emigration as their only future. Tin mining could not absorb the numbers left without work from the copper concerns, and the ministrations of the Poor Law were hardly likely to appeal as an alternative.

As it had done, earlier, in the 1840s and 1850s, the local press carried frequent and detailed reports on the growing tide of emigration. In May 1867, for example, *The West Briton* included the following:

During the last twelve months, Cornish miners to the number of 7,380 have left the county, 1,155 of whom have settled in America, 670 in Australia and New Zealand, 450 in California, while the iron mines of Scotland and the coal and iron mines of the North of England have absorbed 1,090. 1,390 have left the district of Camborne and Redruth; 880, the districts of Gwennap, Stithians, Ilogan and Phillack; 1,590, the districts of Lelant and St Just; 8, the district of Wendron and Sithney; 205, the district of St Austell; and 1,200 the districts of Liskeard and Callington. The returns from the other districts are not so correctly ascertained, but must fall little short of 2,000.

These had been the great centres of copper production, but were now progressively emptying, the communities being forced to go in search of new life elsewhere. There was little enough for those who remained. St Day was the largest community in the great copper mining parish of Gwennap, the richest and most productive district in Cornwall up to the mid-century. *The West Briton* described something of circumstances at St Day in 1878, depression having bitten hard by that time:

Since 1871 six mines have been abandoned in that parish, which at the time employed 3,450 persons. The population in the parish has decreased about twenty per-cent; twelve per-cent of the houses are now unoccupied, and many that are uninhabited are dilapidated; the markets are almost destitute of stalls and are very badly attended; in the last few years one third of the shops have been closed and the shop-keepers who now sell the goods have great difficulty in getting the money.

The great days had gone; the copper miner was either leaving, or had left. Tin mining struggled into the twentieth century and survived, on a limited basis, until quite recently. Cornwall has never fully recovered from its illustrious past, but tourism offered new opportunities and a very different image, drawing upon the rich visual appeal and dramatic character inherent in its antiquities and its mining tradition.

Botallack Mine in 1863 showing men and women at work on the dressing floors set into the cliffside. Beyond, in their almost unique setting, are the engine houses of the Crowns set at the cliff-edge itself. The pumping house is the lower of them, the winding-house, above, being only a matter of seven years old at the time.

Penzance Library

TOURISM AND RAILWAYS – THE TWENTIETH CENTURY

Very early this century, beginning in 1904, the Great Western Railway embarked on what was to become a remarkably successful initiative. They created 'The Cornish Riviera', a masterpiece of inspired imagery and commercial enterprise. As the preface to the first of many GWR publications put it:

> It is becoming every day more and more apparent to all classes of English men and women that, with the Cornish Riviera practically at our doors, the necessity of costly and fatiguing foreign travel exists no longer. The sunny and sheltered littoral of 'The Duchy' rivals, save in the matter of expense, the far-off and much less accessible shores of Southern France or North Africa, or the more distant island of Madeira. (*The Cornish Riviera* 1904)

The decisive note was struck; Cornwall was a priceless possession for the Great Western Railway. The Company spared nothing in its promotion of this exotic, magical land of myth, of legend and history, taking every opportunity to make favourable comparisons with prestigious European and international resorts generally. If initiative and ingenuity frequently out-ran more mundane reality in presenting the delights of the Cornish Riviera, there was little criticism, more, in fact, a willing surrender of sorts to the seductive imagery; not least, in terms of national pride, because it was Britain.

The train journey itself was intended to reflect a special atmosphere, distinction and character. Here, the Great Western made particular reference to its "Much talked of and luxuriantly appointed Express trains," whilst its literary presentations (e.g. the third edition of *The Cornish Riviera*, published in 1908) assured the reader of nothing but the best by "combining literary merit, historic research and antiquarian knowledge with that of artistic skill and all modern improvements in the matters of illustration and presentation." The inter-war era saw the development of powerful images; of mighty and majestic GWR locomotives effortlessly speeding to the West, and of resplendent rolling stock in the positive hierarchy of chocolate and cream livery. These were the hallmarks of standards and service. Handsome locomotives with the distinctive pedigree of King, Castle, Hall Star, and later, Grange and Manor classes, added to a sense of dignity.

Great Western management was anxious to impress upon its passengers that in the actual journey to Cornwall itself they would enjoy a rich and varied spectacle immediately beyond the carriage window. Before then, en-route, was some of the very finest rural landscapes that England could offer; English landscapes, of course; not Cornish. Idyllic pastoral scenes, rich in history, and, by definition, Great Western in their association and character, added immeasurably to the experience of travelling westward, and, of course, increased the overall sense of excitement and anticipation.

Somerset Ways, a GWR publication of the mid-twenties, made the point. Highly representative of the middle-class love of the country and things rural, (always a definitive characteristic of the inter-war years) this extract described the landscape north westward from Somerton to Bridgwater and the Polden Hills. It was a vision of England:

> Here is a county of grass land and orchards; a land of quiet lanes leading to bee-droused farms, where deep-eyed glossy sleek cattle stand contemplative in the tree shade . . . a land of woods and thickets studded with diamond, anemone, and sapphire hyacinth, with delicate white, mauve-veined wood-sorrel lurking among its shamrock leaves followed by foxglove and bracken and the tints of turning bramble. Field paths and stiles are here, leading through ripening corn rustling with every vagrant puff of air, or through knee-high, luscious meadow grass sprinkled with yellow gems of buttercups.

The sea-wall spectacle at Dawlish and Teignmouth provided contrast, adding considerably to the character and appeal of the journey, not to mention its prestige value for the company itself. Further westward again in South Devon, the South Hams district was the subject of another detailed and obvious celebration of the English landscape. Here, as in all this manner of material, the Great Western relished its associations with such images of Britain, seeing itself as an integral part of the community and its character. The extract here is taken from another of the company's books, *Devon: The Shire of Sea Kings*, this second impression being dated March, 1926:

> Between the main line of the Great Western Railway from Totnes to Plymouth and the English Channel lies one of the richest and most prosperous districts of Southern Devon. Rocky headlands, precipitous cliffs, pleasant coves, strangely shaped creeks often

A GWR omnibus service, to and from Penzance station, stands in the Square at St Just. This valuable asset, first introduced in May 1904, was one of many gradually opening out access to the area before World War One. A service to Lands End also began in April 1904. The Lizard was served from Helston with buses operating from the station in August 1903. The G.W.R. opened Coverack Road Motor Halt in 1928 thereby further improving access to the popular Lizard peninsula. Coverack was a particularly attractive fishing community sure to be popular with tourists, and was frequently photographed. *Author's Collection*

Lands End and the Longships Lighthouse. Lands End is invariably the ultimate destination of tourists to West Cornwall. Not necessarily the most outstanding coastline in Cornwall, it is, nevertheless, unique and will continue to attract innumerable visitors, as it has done for centuries. *Cornish Studies Library*

Cape Cornwall, near St Just in the far west. The headland is crowned by the chimney of the former Cape Cornwall Mine. Mining, market gardening and tourism have all made their mark on this distinctive location, facing the Atlantic Ocean.

Cornish Studies Library

Logan Rock, near Porthcurno in the far west of the county. This photograph from the 1920s shows the rock structure at the cliff side, the rock being said to be so finely balanced that it could be, as *Murray's Handbook* put it, "made to oscillate on its point of support." An added attraction at this magnificent coastal site was in the access itself, Logan Rock being within the confines of the ancient Iron Age cliff castle of Treryn Dinas, the largest of its kind in the district.

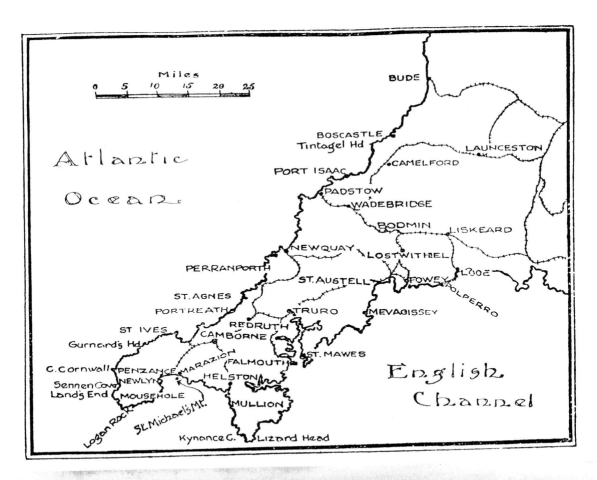

Working the nets. This 1920s view of fishermen at work on the quay at St Ives was just the kind of image that the GWR desired. The combination of the traditional community and that of magnificent golden beaches was certain to attract the tourist.

Cornish Studies Library

reaching far inland, with octopus-like branches, sun-lined 'laps' of golden sand, fruitful orchards, giant elms and oaks, hedgerows aglow with wild flowers, smiling meadows and sequestered 'coombes' where lemons and oranges ripen in the open air and blue hydrangeas lie in masses under the trees, such are some of the distinctive features of the fertile South Hams . . . Picturesque villages, interesting churches, creeper-covered cottages and venerable manor houses, old world inns and an abundance of legend and folk-lore, add very materially to the attractions with which generous nature has endowed this particular part of the Devonian Riviera . . .

This was Devon at its best, but for all its obvious appeal the West Country was always a part of England, to be compared with other magnificent landscapes, as in the Cotswolds or the Welsh Marches; all good Great Western territory. Cornwall was different; it was mysterious, unique, and comparisons were made, not with other British resorts, but with acknowledged and acclaimed locations overseas.

May 1925 saw the publication of *The Ocean Coast*, a book to promote the numerous coastal resorts served by the GWR from Weymouth, on the Dorset coast, to Pwllheli on Cardigan Bay. For obvious reasons, Cornwall was given special place: "The Ocean Coast climate" it argued, "is most perfectly exemplified in Cornwall because that county is almost entirely surrounded by sea. Unless it comes straight down one narrow neck of land, every wind must be a sea wind."

The climate – often described as semi-tropical – offered everything for the summer visitor; it also appealed to those seeking a winter retreat, this being one of its particular attractions. Beyond this, however, *The Ocean Coast* struck a characteristic theme of that period, namely, the escape from an urban, industrial environment into something altogether more exciting and wholesome. The literature of escape and adventure, be it on temporary or permanent basis, had considerable following for those with the means to indulge in it between the Wars:

The Ocean Coast is as entirely desirable as a place of residence as it is indispensable for a holiday.

More and more people are realising this. All round the western coast tiny colonies are coming into being, new suburbs are fringing the big resorts, and groups of bungalows and modern houses are appearing in seaward coombes. All – or nearly all – are the new, long dreamed of homes of those who have earned their rest, and have gone to the warm and sunny ocean coast to enjoy it.it is a move worth making. It means much more than renewed health, more than the return to your walk of that spring you lost – you thought you lost for ever – ten, fifteen or twenty years ago.

To live where the sun and the soft sea air are imparts a new flavour and relish to the whole of life. To watch the change from dusk to starlight over the gently swaying waters, to watch the slower change from spring to summer in some western valley brings to the watcher a peace and contentment that modern cities have banished from their walls. Away from the roar and clatter of industrialism our senses come back to us. The hurry of modern life falls off like a discarded garment, and with it falls many an haunting fear, many a petty irritation, and many a narrowing prejudice. We begin again to 'see life clear and see it whole.'

Hand in hand with this comes a physical change every bit as wonderful. Nerves are soothed and steadied, tissues cleaned and revitalised by sun and wind, soon you begin to get that sound sleep each night, that glad awakening each morning that you thought belonged to youth alone.

The whole of life becomes sweet as a hazel-nut.

Whilst the author of *The Ocean Coast* may have lacked the literary style and flourish of the Great Western's best writers one could easily be forgiven for thinking that no less a person than Stanley Baldwin might have penned such lines. His fulsome praise of all things rural whilst living in and overseeing as prime minister an advanced industrial state (albeit one in considerable difficulties), certainly had something in common with the situation of the GWR. One of the most interesting features of the Great Western between the Wars was its concern, on the one hand to be seen to be modern, progressive and in step with the times generally, whilst, on the other, seeking support, reference and increasing refuge in the past, and the traditions of Old England, with its history, people and culture, when it came to tourism and leisure.

It is also important to remember that the GWR itself was a large and successful business, promoting and serving industry, part of the process which, at times, it criticised. The conflict, of course, was part of a national consciousness. It represented something of the reaction against aspects of urban development and the pressures of an industrial society, and was well reflected in the fact that the English countryside and all things rural found the strongest support and best expression amongst the comfortable and increasingly leisured, middle-class urban population. All this, at a time when agriculture was in a deeply depressed condition. The inter-war years were, indeed, interesting times, full of fascinating irony.

Not surprisingly, literature produced by the Great Western Railway abounded in images of Cornwall as the location every bit as favourable as the prestigious watering places of the Continent. Unlike other West Country areas, largely portrayed in terms of lush rural imagery, Cornwall was linked closely with the sea and with exotic and stylish settings, heavily romantic.

The Cornish Riviera 1904, the Company's first promotional work, had this to say of Penzance:

> The pilgrim to Penzance in search of either health, rest or change need have no fear of dullness. If he walks in the Morrab Gardens, where a good band plays amongst a wealth of sub-tropical vegetation which Nice or Monte Carlo might envy, he may without any stretch of the imagination fancy himself in Algiers.

St Ives was another of the Cornish resorts certain to be given this treatment, as in *The Cornish Riviera* of 1924. 'No part of the coast feels the direct effect of the Gulf Stream more distinctly, for many have been the instances of West Indian drift cast upon the shores of its lovely bay.'

An entirely new edition of *The Cornish Riviera*, especially written by S. P. Mais, and published by the GWR in August 1928, maintained the comparisons with the fashionable resorts overseas:

> Penzance is proving a formidable rival to Madeira, the Scillies, to the Azores and Mullion to Monte Carlo.

Together with these gems, Mais further developed the theme that Cornwall was not England. He wrote of bridges, countries and cream:

> Scotsmen are proud and rightly proud of their magnificent Forth Bridge, but they cannot pretend as the visitor crosses from South to North Queensferry that he is changing one country for another, Brunel's Royal Albert Bridge at Saltash, majestic and picturesque as it is, cannot compare in length with the bridge over the Firth of Forth, but it is the means, an almost magical means of transporting travellers from a county, which, if richer than others is yet unmistakably an English county, to a Duchy which is in every respect un-English. You shut your eyes going over the Saltash Bridge only to open them again on a foreign scene, Cornish cream is not Devonshire cream; the Cornish people are not English people.

Newquay became Cornwall's leading and best known resort, and like all the Cornish holiday centres, it owed much in its growth and reputation to the railway. (See later section for fuller treatment of Newquay). It also best exemplified the imagery, the aspirations and ideals set out in the extract from *The Ocean Coast* quoted above. The magnificent beaches were there, parks and gardens offering the important element of gentility had been laid out, and there were, of course, the inevitable golf links. The coastline certainly provided all the grandeur, drama, and romance that those in search of atmosphere and inspiration could desire.

An extract from the *Homeland Handbook*, always a useful source for the Great Western's writers, conveyed the magic and moods of Bedruthan Steps, a much visited coastal location, near Mawgan Porth, between Newquay and Padstow:

> The best photographs fail to give any adequate idea of this beautiful bay. The cliffs towering to an altitude of fully three hundred feet seen against a background of blue sky, are rugged and wild beyond description. In winter and early spring before the season of gales is quite over, it is no uncommon thing to see a mast or some other bit of wreckage tossed by the breakers in their mad fury half-way up these storm-beaten heights . . .
>
> Down on the sands are giant rocks covered with shells, blue-grey mussels bristling thickly and countless beautiful varieties of the homely winkle of commerce, from the full nondescript hue of the well-known edible, to saffron colour, rose, soft sea green, white and palest grey. The rock pools are just as clear and pure as the air and faithfully reflect all this irridescence of colouring, as well as the outlines of the monitor rocks,

weathered to all sorts of strange shapes.
This was the Cornwall that brought the GWR such unreserved pride.

Newquay's magnificent beaches, in views from the early years of this century. The first shows Towan Beach in the foreground with Great Western and Tolcarne beyond.

Towan was described in the early days as the least of the three, "chiefly used as an early bathing place by gentlemen visitors." Great Western considered to be the main beach, was "monopolised by bathers of the gentler sex from nine in the morning until three in the afternoon." Tolcarne Beach was generally set aside for men's bathing – access was not easy.

The second view shows bathers enjoying their time on the sands – note their costumes and the Atlantic Hotel on the cliff beyond. There was great controversy over the plans for the Headland Hotel overlooking Fistral Beach. Many people opposed the development of the headland area, giving rise to active protest, obstruction and demonstration.   *Cornish Studies Library*

THE CORNISH RIVIERA

FOREWORD.

THE Cornish Riviera possesses all the climatic advantages once considered the attribute of Madeira, Southern France and Italy, Algeria, and the still more distant Delta of the Nile, while the "Delectable Duchy" generally has been more than once described as "the playground *par excellence* of the British Empire." The beauty and variety of its scenery are as remarkable as the richness of its historical associations, which go back to times even more remote than those in which the Phœnicians came from Carthage to Cornwall in quest of tin.

Cornwall is not only celebrated for the picturesqueness of its indented coast line and the rugged beauty of its rocks, cliffs and uplands, but at every turn the traveller finds himself face to face with venerable cairns and cromlechs, with ancient wells and moss-grown crosses, and with churches and other buildings, the origin of which is often shrouded in mystery. It is in Cornwall only that the memorials of our Celtic ancestors can be satisfactorily explored, and recent developments of railway travel carried out by the Holiday Line of England enable holiday-makers to do in a few days or hours more than could formerly be accomplished in weeks or even months.

No. 1 THE CORNISH RIVIERA AND ITS
— CLIMATE. —

NO clearer or more succinct summary of the general meteorological characteristics of Cornwall can be found than that which the late Mr. Nicholas Whiteley, C.E., supplied, in words which cannot be too widely known: "A Canadian would think there was no summer and say there was no winter . . . . [so far removed are the climatic conditions of Cornwall from extremes]. The month of January at Penzance is as warm as at Madrid, Florence, and Constantinople; and July is as cool as at St. Petersburg in that month. The seasons appear to mingle like the interlacing of the warm and cold waters on the edge of the Gulf Stream; and along our coast line, in January, night and day have hardly a distinctive temperature. There is no country in the world with a climate so mild and equable as the south-west of England, if we except the south-west of Ireland, where this peculiarity is intensified. The cause is now well understood. The Atlantic Ocean on the west is an immense reservoir of warm water, fed and heated by the Gulf Stream, so that around the Cornish land in the depth of winter the temperature of the surface water is seldom lower than 46°, and out at sea, beyond the influence of the land, the water is much warmer."

Extracts from *The Scenery, Attractions and Historical Associations of the Cornish Riviera* – GWR, 1913

Further north, there were the mysteries of Tintagel and Boscastle, rich in the mythology folk-lore and legend of King Arthur, and ancient days, whilst at the opposite end of the county, off the south coast, was St Michael's Mount. The Mount figured very largely in Great Western posterwork and was described as one of the "Seven Wonders of England," by S. P. Mais in *The Cornish Riviera* .

Not known for understatement, Mais wrote elsewhere that the Isles of Scilly were for him, "close to the idea the Garden of Eden." But his work had vigour, character and, of course, an unmistakable commitment, well suited to GWR interests and to that elusive element, 'the spirit of the age.' Not surprisingly, Mais presented St Michael's Mount in terms of a unique experience and, therefore, everything that the prospective tourist could ask for; certainly nothing less than the Great Western Railway would have expected:

> From far or near, in whatever weather, at whatever time of day, St. Michael's Mount stands out as one of the Seven Wonders of England, mysterious, exquisitely beautiful a citadel of romance on which to base the castle of dreams. I had myself the great good fortune to see it first at midnight under a harvest moon with its lights in high walls flashing over the seas. I have seen it emerge above a sea-mist like a magic place on the clouds; I have seen it with the storms beating great waves against its granite sides, and I have seen it shimmering in the noon-day heat of a perfect midsummer day. Each time it has seemed beyond compare, the most exquisite gem of all England's homes.

St Michael's Mount with Marazion, the mainland community in the foreground. This photograph from 1935 shows the Mount in relation to the shoreline, together with the causeway linking them and nearby Chapel Rock.

Monastery, Castle, Stately Home, and deservedly one of Britain's most famous tourist attractions, St Michael's Mount is steeped in history, legend and romance. Not surprisingly the Great Western Railway made it a centre piece, a focus for much of their publicity for Cornwall.   *Penzance Library*

Looking beyond the mainland to the Isles of Scilly, there were further celebrations of landscape and climate. Great Western publicity was concerned to stress the attraction and exclusive appeal of the islands, whilst carefully emphasising company commitment to the highest standards of service. As *The Cornish Riviera* of 1908 put it:

> If you are in a hurry, leave Paddington at 9 p.m., enjoy a comfortable night's rest in the sleeping car and wake up in time to catch a passing glance of 'Majestic Michael.' Breakfast at your leisure in Penzance in a sunny room overlooking Mounts Bay; go on board and lunch luxuriantly on the S.S. Lyonesse.

John Wesley considered the Islands "a barren, dreary place" in the mid eighteenth century, but later writers saw things differently, often being at a loss to express the beauty and fascination of the place. Walter Besant's *Armorel of Lyonesse*, a useful reference for GWR material, offered up enticing images of luxuriant growth, fulsome and sensuous:

> You cannot go picking pepper here, nor can you strip the cinnamon tree of its bark. But here you will see the bamboos cluster tall and graceful; the eucalyptus here parades his naked trunk and blue leaves; here the fern tree lifts its circle of glory of lace and embroidery 20 feet high; the prickly pear nestles in warm corners; the aloe shoots up its tall stalk of flower and seed; the palms stand in long rows and every lovely plant, every sweet flower created for the solace of man grows abundantly, and hastens with zeal to display its blossoms; the soft air is full of perfumes, strange and familiar: it is as if Kew had taken off her glass roofs and placed all her plants and trees to face the English winter.

Looking to the shores and the definitive presence of the sea, Besant sustained the idyll:

> Here a bay in which the water, on such days as it could be approached, peacefully laps a smooth white beach; here dark caves and holes in which the water even on the calmest days of summer, grumbles and groans, and when the least sea rises, begin to bellow and roar. In time of storm it shrieks and howls . . . All round the rocks at low tide hangs the long seaweed, undisturbed since the days when they manufactured kelp, like the rank growth of tropical creepers. At high tide it stands erect, rocking to and fro in the wash and sway of the water like tree tops of the forest in a breeze. Everywhere, except in the rare places where man comes and goes, the wild sea-birds make their nests.

The romance and drama of the seas, stunning beaches of white sand and exotic gardens could scarcely fail to impress all who visited the Islands. As *The Cornish Riviera* emphasised, this was a place to take "such a hold of the imagination and the affections that it can never be forgotten or lost."

In completing its coverage of the Islands in the 1924 publication; *Historic Sites and Scenes of England*, the GWR carefully combined themes of mystery legend, great beauty and unique location "at the western-most point of England":

> It is in the fitness of things that the great romance of the days of chivalry should end

The 'Scillonian' in Penzance Harbour in the late 1920s. Entering service early in 1926 the "Scillonian" worked to and from St Mary's for thirty years during which time it carried countless tourists and vast consignments of flowers and market produce, as well as the islands' supplies from the mainland. Isles of Scilly Steamship services were well advertised by the GWR who actively promoted the attractios of the islands throughout its literature.

Cornish Studies Library

LYONESSE:
A HANDBOOK
TO THE
Isles of Scilly.

BY
J. C. TONKIN
AND
B. P. ROW.

Fully Illustrated.

WITH
MAPS.

WITH INTRODUCTION BY
SIR WALTER BESANT.

Price 6d. Nett.

GUIDE TO THE ISLES OF SCILLY

Covers from two late nineteenth-century handbooks.

Tregarthen Hotel, St Marys, Isles of Scilly at the turn of the century. The hotel featured prominently in the GWR's publicity and, specifically, in *The Cornish Riviera*, being described there as the "oldest established and largest hotel on the islands."

Cornish Studies Library

Tresco Abbey gardens showing the palm trees and luxuriant growth that has long characterised the Isles of Scilly. These gardens on Tresco were rightly celebrated as unique to Britain giving the visitor the closest approximation to the atmosphere of the sub-tropical regions. This turn of the century view would have been ideal for GWR publicity for the islands.

Cornish Studies Library

amongst its rocks, its sapphire sea and fields of narcissi, even if the echoes of the fabled bells of the churches lying buried fathoms deep below the waves do not actually reach your ear.

Another favourite theme particularly for GWR poster work was that of the traditional Cornish fishing village. There were many to choose from: – Looe, Polperro, Mevagissey, Fowey, St Ives, Mousehole, Sennen, Port Isaac – all of them fulfilling the appropriate imagery. Seagulls, nets, knowing fishermen and narrow streets; a chaos of houses, cellars and studios; the water's edge, the solidity and permanence of the harbour itself and the boats at their moorings, all such things contributed immensely to the character and diversity of experience that defined the Cornish Riviera.

The GWR played a decisive part in the development of tourism in Cornwall and in the West of England overall. The carefully created image of a unique setting distinguished from other parts of Britain in terms of its landscape, climate and culture was an undoubted commercial success. Critics of this steady popularisation, perhaps, even exploitation of Cornwall, argued that in many respects the substance and vigour of the traditional way of life was gradually being replaced by a powerful seductive image, which, for all its appeal amounted to no more than a semblance of reality.

The *Homeland Handbook* took up the closely related theme of the nature of tourism and tourists, and the question of the real identity and true character of Cornwall. This was to become a very real issue for the twentieth century, and in raising the debate, the writer drew out some extremely telling comparisons and contrasts. Past and present, time and place, and the qualitative presence of landscape and history, the 'spirit' or dramatic impact of the county, was effectively set out against the vastly different considerations of the priorities and the style of early twentieth century tourism. As ever, with the *Homeland Handbook,* there was no theoretical discussion, no formal debate or lecture, the issues were presented through the narrative, through the powerful appeal of atmosphere and ethos; image and event, routine and romance:

In these days of universal travel thousands of people visit the 'delectable duchy' every year. They climb the Cheesewring, picnic amongst the ruins of Tintagel's hoary keep, explore the sylvan beauties of the Fal, and stand on Old Bolerion (West Penwith) and strain their eye to catch a glimpse of the long, low, uneven silhouette of the Scillies. Then when their holidays are over, they go home and tell their friends of a land of vivid colouring and rocky grandeur. They speak enthusiastically of palm trees, of geraniums, twenty feet high, of fuchsias that grow like large shrubs, of wild asparagus and other vegetarian wonders. They compare with a sneer the pea-green water of the English Channel to the sapphire rollers of the Atlantic and assert that after the pinnacles headlands of the west, the chalk cliffs of the south coast look like neatly cut white cheese.

But how many of these people know the real uniqueness of Cornwall? Very few. For this land of primeval solitudes and prehistoric monuments is not to be discovered in a few weeks of sight-seeing. Its true spirit does not reveal itself on the sea fronts of its watering places, or in the show spots of the guide books.

In order to really know Cornwall it is necessary to leave the beaten tracks and follow the less trodden paths of her moors and cliffs, to trace the little moorland streams from source to sea, to discover those quaint grey villages that nestle in the hollow of the hills and to make the acquaintance of warm-hearted, quick-witted Celtic inhabitants. To this day England may be said to terminate on the shores of the Tamar. Beyond this river is a land of legend and mystery, of eloquent silences and Homeric storms . . .

The Penwith highlands reach almost to Lands End and in many ways are the most arresting of all the Cornish uplands. Nowhere else in the Duchy will you find a grander coastline, a wilder, more picturesque moorland or such a wealth of prehistoric villages, burial sites and stone circles. This is the sanctum of the Cornish Celt. Here you will find him clinging to his granite hillside, still listening to the song of the sea and the moan of the moorland wind.

Focussing in upon the moors north of Penzance, between the site of the abandoned Ding Dong Mine and the north coast itself, below Carn Galver and Bosigran Cliffs, the Handbook continued:

All around us now are prehistoric remains; for we are in the land of long ago, the unchanged home of a vanished people whose monuments still survive. To the east, cutting the sky-line of a long hill are the engine houses of the disused Ding Dong Mine, one of the oldest in Cornwall. Their slender stacks point upwards like the index finger of a giant hand. They serve no purpose now except as nesting places for kestrels. Ivy is creeping over the gaunt walls which seem curiously in harmony with nature and the wild spirit of the moor. They have been adopted by the wilderness in a way few buildings could be . . . Then there is the silence that envelops one's soul and seems to raise it above the fret and fame of a money grabbing world. A silence rendered more impressive by the tiny cataracts of song from the soaring larks and the murmur or innumerable bees.

Fortunately, many might say, in spite of the intense development of twentieth century tourism, one can, today, still enjoy this particular image of Cornwall to the full. The mine, the prehistoric stone circles and the primeval moorland remains. Overlooked by the mysterious and brooding Carn Galver, this landscape, as with much of the coastline, has always offered the experience of unrivalled natural beauty and grandeur, but also here, perhaps, a relationship with the landscape itself.

In fact, the process of the 'discovery' of Cornwall began long before the popular commercial initiatives of the Great Western Railway. Looking at literature from the mid-nineteenth century, in this case, *Rambles Beyond Railways*, written by Wilkie Collins and published in 1861, the Cornish coastline is described in irresistible manner, clearly setting the style for later Great Western material. There is a nice irony in the title of Collins's book; if anything, it was certain to encourage the railway presence. These final extracts, which could so easily have been adopted by the GWR, some forty or so years later, express all those elements of drama and of powerfully romantic location certain to appeal to the traveller in search of experience and place.

Wilkie Collins was much impressed by the Lizard peninsula, particularly by Kynance Cove where he claimed that this district's coastal scenery "arrives at its climax of grandeur":

What a scene was now presented to us! It was a perfect palace of rocks! Some rose perpendicularly and separate from each other, in the shape of pyramids and steeples – some were overhanging at the top and pierced with dark caverns at the bottom – some were stretched horizontally on the sand, here studded with pools of water, there broken into natural archways. No one of these rocks resembled another in shape, size, or position . . .

Collins went on to offer the reader the sensations of close proximity to the elements relating the drama, atmosphere and exilharation therein:

The tide is rising fast. The sea dashes in higher and higher waves on the narrowing beach. Rain and mist are gone. overhead, the clouds are falling asunder in every direction assuming strange momentary shapes, quaint airy resemblances of the forms of great rocks among which we stand. height after height along the distant cliffs dawn on us gently; the great golden rays shoot down over them; far out on the ocean, the waters flash into a streak of fire; the sails of ships passing there glitter bright; yet a moment more, and the glorious sunlight bursts out over the whole view. The sea changes soon from dull grey to bright blue, embroidered thickly with golden specks, as it rolls and rushes and dances in the wind. The sand at our feet grows brighter and purer to the eye; the sea birds flying and swooping above us look like flashes of white light against the blue firmament; and most beautiful of all, the wet serpentine rocks now shine forth in full splendour beneath the sun; everyone of their exquisite varieties of colour becomes plainly visible – silver grey and bright yellow, dark red, deep brown, and malachite green appear . . . glorious ornaments of the seashore, fashioned by no human art! Nature's home-made jewelry, which the wear of centuries has failed to tarnish, and the rage of tempests has been powerless to destroy.

Who after all, could resist this? Not many, it seems, judging by the countless thousands, this century, more than happy to heed the Company's advice to "Go Great Western" to the delights of the "Cornish Riviera."

Opposite:
Kynance as photographed in the 1920s – the kind of illustration one would have found in GWR coaching stock right through until the early 1960s.

The fishing fleet at rest in Polperro Harbour in the days when the port had a substantial number of boats – sailing craft as shown here. This photograph, from the inter-war years, shows the beginnings of residential development, and, with this, the gradual and inexorable challenge to its traditional character. Visited by John Wesley in the eighteenth century, a thriving fishing community in the nineteenth century, Polperro has become an obvious attraction for tourists this century.

Cornish Studies Library

THE GWR AND NEWQUAY

Newquay's earliest experience of railways dated from 1849 when the industrialist J. T. Treffry opened two lines, one from the St Dennis district, inland, the other from East Wheal Rose mine near Newlyn East. These lines made the vital link with the sea, developing Newquay as a small but useful port. Passenger services waited on later days and a very different railway system in the shape of the Cornwall Minerals Railway of the 1870s.

The Cornwall Minerals line linked Newquay with Par and the deep-water port of Fowey on the south coast. Freight traffic – iron ore at first, later, china clay – began on 1st June 1874; passenger services were introduced two years later.

Newquay Tourist Traffic

'We feel sure that the extension of the railway system to Newquay will attract thousands of visitors to our beautiful beaches and magnificent cliffs, and materially contribute to the prosperity of the neighbourhood.'

With this and other similar statements the people of Newquay officially welcomed the beginning of passenger services to the town on 20th July 1876. The first train started from Fowey on the Tuesday morning and was greeted with celebrations all along the line. As always, there were the local dignitaries, including Mr Richardson, the CMR General Manager, and Mr Constantine, the locomotive superintendent who drove the train. The St Blazey Band joined the train at Par to travel to Newquay , and at Victoria (Roche) the local school children were assembled on one platform and the general public on the other. A salute of fog signals was arranged and the vicar read an 'Address', welcoming the new service. At Newquay the train received 'a perfect ovation'; the entire community turning out to welcome, including the Foresters and Oddfellows, the coastguard and lifeboatmen.

The Cornwall Minerals Railway, in opening their services, also expressed optimism, predicting that 'under favourable circumstances, Newquay would become a second Torquay'. As a potential resort, Newquay had a great deal to recommend it. With the direct support of the Great Western Railway, who worked the CMR system from 1st October 1877, controlling it outright from 1st July 1896, tourism made good progress. The train service for 1876 is given here.

Prior to the opening of the connecting curve, brought into use of 1st January 1879, an omnibus service was provided for passengers between the Cornwall Railway's station and that of the CMR at Par. The timetable was also designed to give the best possible connections for 'up' and 'down' trains on the Cornwall line. The early departure from Newquay, for example, connected with the Paddington service which arrived at Par at 8.04 and Paddington at 6 p.m.

Before the introduction of passenger services to Newquay, the GWR promoted a four horse bus service (1st May 1876) from Newquay to St Columb conveying passengers and mail. The coach then connected with a further service to Grampound Road station on the main line with a return working provided during the evening. The GWR arranged facilities for passengers to book at Newquay or St Columb for any station on its system.

The last quarter of the nineteenth century saw important steps in the transformation of Newquay from a small fishing and trading community into a recognised resort. A gas company was formed in 1878, and a water company four years later. A detailed sanitary programme also got under way during 1875 as part of the plan to create a modern, fashionable centre, the Local Board of Health receiving £3,000 from the Public Works Loan Commissioners to finance improvements. Further substantial developments with regard to water supply, drainage and sanitation also took effect at the turn of the century and in the years immediately prior to World War One. Much of Newquay's water supply was actually brought to the town in pipes laid along the course of the railway line itself; the source being located inland near Indian Queens.

By 1911 Newquay had a population of 4,415; in contrast, it had been 1,121 in 1871. Housing and hotels flourished. The best known hotels were the Atlantic, dating from 1890. The Great Western, 1878, The Hotel Victoria, 1899, the only hotel in England providing electric lifts from all floors to the beach below, and The Headland, 'the largest hotel in the West of England'. For its part, the GWR contributed £2,000 towards hotel development; the more exclusive accommodation mentioned here emphasising the modern amenities; electric lighting and lifts, telephones, 'the best sanitation' and attractions such as tennis, bowling greens, golf and the important proximity to the beaches. Significantly, the rateable value at Newquay increased from £5,050 in 1883 to £32,244 in 1914.

Queen Bess Rock, Bedruthan Steps, near Newquay – a magnificent coastal setting where the atmosphere was everything that the GWR could hope for in its promotion of the celebrated "Ocean Coast."

Cornish Studies Library

Newquay also had its obvious attractions for the rival London and South Western Railway. Their own publication *By Cornish Sea and Moors*, produced in 1915, gave full details of their services linking with North Cornwall. The North Cornwall Coach Company conveyed passengers between Wadebridge and Newquay and also offered access to the 'romantic scenery' of Boscastle and Tintagel rich in the Arthurian legend.

Boscastle Harbour on the north coast. Castle Boterel, as it was named by Thomas Hardy in his novels and poetry, was and will always be a wildly dramatic location full of the romance of cliff and sea. Magnificent in summer weather and awesome in winter this was the coastline of "haunted heights, where the blind gales sweep."
Cornish Studies Library

A useful addition to traffic locally came with the opening of the GWR Chacewater - Newquay branch via St Agnes and Perranporth on 2nd January 1905. This line did a great deal to open out tourism in West Cornwall giving good access to other resorts like Falmouth, Penzance and St Ives. it also played its part in what the 'West Briton' referred to as 'Newquay's second birth'. The town obviously felt a great sense of pride and achievement in the opening of the new line. In response to new opportunities the 'West Briton' recorded:

'Newquay people realise that the time for extra effort has arrived. The Council in turning its attention to the provision of a public park, and the scheme at Trenance Valley which has been under consideration for a couple of years is being hurried forward. The town is not encumbered by any debt and can afford to launch forth. The electric light is also to be installed by a private company.'

The terminus also benefited from substantial improvements to coincide with the opening of the Chacewater route and the increase in traffic from other parts of Britain. A new island platform was provided enabling three trains to use the station when required; passenger facilities generally were also improved together with the extra provision for goods and locomotive sheds. A figure of £30,000 was given for these developments. Tolcarne Junction was also realigned (1904) with the addition of two sections of double track with loops; one section serving the route to Par, and the other, the new line to Perranporth and Chacewater.

Intermediate stations on the 20¾ mile section from Par and the main line were progressively renamed, with the exception of Bugle. Halloon became St Columb Road in December 1878, whilst Par, on the CMR, was renamed St Blazey in January 1879; Bridges became Luxulyan in May 1905 and Holywell became Victoria, and, finally, Roche in November 1904. Quintrell Downs was opened by the GWR in October 1911. All the stations had passing loops with the exception of the latter.

The shoreline at Perranporth. With its dramatic combination of cliffs, island outcrops and wide expanse of beach, this former mining community grew to become an important tourist resort particularly with the opening of the GWR branch service in 1903. It is yet another of the infinite variations on the Ocean Coast theme.

Cornish Studies Library

Finally, before leaving the formative years of the line, it needs to be said that prior to 1st January 1879 there were no effective links at all between the GWR and the CMR at Par. On that date a half mile curve was opened linking Par GWR with the minerals line yet until May 1892 and the abolition of the broad gauge, standard gauge 'branch' trains to Newquay stood alongside broad gauge main line services at Par. The removal of the broad gauge allowed through running to Newquay adding to the attraction for tourists, and encouraging the GWR to plan more ambitious services to and from the resort.

The inter-war years marked further progress enabling Newquay to establish itself as the county's premier tourist resort. Expenditure on publicity gave a good indication of growth. in 1926 for example, the town spent £130 on advertising; by 1935, with the direct assistance of the GWR this figure had risen to £1,000, this being considerably more than that of any other Cornish resort. Newquay's population was well over 8,000 by this time, being a community which, again, unlike other local resorts, was largely committed to a tourist economy. The Chamber of Commerce acknowledged the efforts of the GWR in stating that the company had 'taught them the use of advertising'. Newquay was also concerned with the 'Come to Cornwall Association', another initiative linked with the GWR dating from the 1920s. This encouraged a collective concern on the part of the resorts to promote tourism within the county.

The small Towan promenade was improved in 1928 with the provision of a theatre and shelters. This helped to open out access to the sea in the immediate town area. There were magnificent sea views from the headlands and cliffs beyond the town, but Newquay has always lacked a lengthy promenade like those at Falmouth and Penzance.

Publicity was all important. In 1938 members of the national and provincial press were invited to Newquay to promote the 'Easter Holiday Campaign', largely influenced by the GWR in order to extend the season more widely.

Holiday Haunts for 1938 shows representative third class monthly returns to Newquay as follows:–

Paddington	49s 1d
Birmingham	47s 9d
Sheffield	60s 11d
Manchester	61s 11d

Holiday Runabout tickets were also available on a weekly basis, together with an extra service, the 'Specimen Newquay Tour'. This was as follows:

Saturday:
> To Newquay, transfer to hotel, weekend at leisure.

Monday:
> Whole day tour to Lands End/St Ives with luncheon at Lands End Hotel.

Tuesday:
> At leisure in Newquay.

Wednesday:
> Whole day tour to Looe and Polperro by coach.

Thursday & Friday:
> At leisure in Newquay.

Saturday:
> Return home train.

The introduction of the Holidays with Pay Act of 1938 proved an important development particularly for the post-war years when tourism flourished at Newquay. Success as a resort was by this time an imperative. Of all the Cornish tourist centres Newquay was now the most important; it was also unique in as far as its economy was almost entirely linked to the holiday industry. The population of the Newquay Urban District had grown by 8.2 per 1,000 per annum between 1931 and 1939 as against a static situation at Penzance and increases at Truro and Falmouth of 3.6 and 1.9. The neighbouring area, particularly villages such as Cubert and Newlyn East, also grew rapidly between the two Wars, indicating the popularity of the area. Nearby Holywell Bay also grew as a resort. Census returns for the thirty year period 1931-61 further reflected Newquay's growth; – 1931 – 7,651; 1951 – 9,930; 1961 – 11,881.

The branch and the terminus itself were also improved with the development of tourism. The Goonbarrow Junction to Bugle section was provided with double track from July 1930, and Bugle station was rebuilt on a new alignment. The crossing loops at all the stations, except, of course, Quintrell Downs, were lengthened considerably during the 1930s whilst, earlier, in August 1921, the section from Tregoss Moor to St Dennis Junction was doubled. This latter section was to the east of St Dennis Junction itself and was almost two miles long.

Newquay station was further extended and the yard enlarged to cope with the increased summer traffic, work beginning in 1938. World War Two delayed things but by March 1946 the section from Tolcarne Junction into Newquay station was doubled, and a new signalbox was provided off the end of the new platforms, to the west of the line. The triangle at Tolcarne had been reinstated in 1931 to enable tender locomotives to turn, the section involved, being the old east curve that originally gave direct access from the Fowey direction into the line to Shepherds and the mining district. One further major improvement to the branch must be recorded this being the rebuilding of Trenance viaduct, immediately outside Newquay. During 1938/1939 the single track structure here was replaced by a double track masonry viaduct built around the earlier stone piers.

The GWR planned to spend altogether some £80,000 at the terminus in carrying out its extension programme. Land was to be purchased on both sides of the line in the station area, and, on the west side of the line, over the whole distance to Tolcarne Junction. The platforms were extended, as at Penzance, to accommodate the heaviest holiday trains that the line could carry, and the original station yard and goods area was remodelled and extended to provide the necessary siding space for holiday trains. Should it be necessary, the yard could offer eleven lines for coaching stock, the seven most westerly of these being the main accommodation.

Tourist traffic increased considerably in the post-war period, the 1938 Holidays with Pay Act proving a major incentive, Newquay certainly had a great deal to offer its visitors in the shape of its magnificent beaches, coastal scenery, parks, gardens and recreational features – theatre, cinema, boating, golfing and tennis. Its popularity, however, gave rise to serious discussion on improvements to transport. In the late 1930s there were considerations of a regular air service and detailed concern about the development of the road system; there were also telling criticisms of rail services. heavy summer trains frequently required not only double-heading but banking also. The improvements of the inter-war years eased traffic problems, but the severe limitations of a mineral line imposed working restrictions that could not be entirely overcome short of reconstruction. In fact, the local press carried details of a suggested scheme discussed by the GWR for a new line, as was the case with the Looe branch.

Rail services were not, however, seriously challenged until the late 1950s by which time holiday traffic on the branch had reached its peak.

The line continues to enjoy its distinction of being the only Cornish branch to carry through services in the summer months, but traffic over the branch in winter is sparse. All the intermediate stations along the line are now no more than unstaffed halts whilst Newquay itself reflects both times present and past. Of the platforms extended to meet heavy traffic requirements between the wars, one is now ruinous beyond the main station area, the other, the island platform, has lost its canopy. The sidings have been shortened to make way for the inevitable car park, whilst outside, on the main road, the railway presence has all but disappeared; the station entrance now forming part of an anonymous modern street development.

Lawson's Motors, a Scottish coaching business, seen here with an excursion at Lands End in 1938. The famous 'First and Last House', and, beyond it again, the coastline at Cape Cornwall is also well illustrated here. Coach travel was beginning to make an impact on the traditional railway market in tourism by this time. *Penzance Library*

The London and South Western, later to become part of the Southern Railway's empire, made its particular impact on North Cornwall. Whilst it never had influence across the county on the scale of the GWR, the London South Western's presence was registered early in the railway era through its interest in the pioneering Bodmin and Wadebridge Railway, dating from 1834. but it was the arrival of through services on the North Cornwall line from Halwill Junction, entering the county at Launceston, thence striking across country to Camelford, Delabole, Wadebridge and, eventually, Padstow in 1899, that marked the most significant progress here. Further north, the LSWR increased its influence with the opening of the Bude branch, also forming a junction with the Wadebridge and Padstow line at Halwill Junction, deep in rural Devon. The line opened to Bude, from Holsworthy, in August 1898.

Porth Gaverne – the coastline near Port Isaac. A view along this North Cornish cliff showing the sweeping grandeur of the scene, "the dark colouring of the cliffs, a wide and beautiful undulating landscape," and, of course, the restless might of the Atlantic itself. All these were seized upon by the two rival railway companies, seeking to promote the county via the Ocean Coast ideal and the prestigious appeal of the 'Atlantic Coast Express'.

Cornish Studies Library

Tintagel Castle – The magical seat of Arthur and the setting for the story of Camelot, or so we are led to believe, by the many poets and writers drawn by the stories of this ancient king and his fabulous court. If ever Arthur and his queen, the Knights of the Round Table and Merlin, the Magician, walked the earth, this should surely have been the famed Camelot. The poetic truth, if disputed by historical accuracy, holds great sway in the remarkably atmospheric cliff-top setting.

Cornish Studies Library

Padstow – "One of the quaintest oddest little towns in all the kingdom," as the *Homeland Handbook* put it. Padstow developed as a fishing port well into this century, ably assisted by the London and South Western, later, Southern Railway. The community was said to bear a strong resemblance in character and appearance to "some continental seaport" or locations resonant of "Madeira, Sack or Canary."

Cornish Studies Library

Both Padstow and Bude made superb holiday resorts, acting as tourist centres for their particular districts, but neither line served any significant population or industries. Padstow dealt with some large traffic in fish, for example, and the rural nature of the area gave rise to related agricultural traffic, but extensive prosperity was never the case in North Cornwall.

Tourism, however, made particular headway as North Cornwall had a great deal to offer. The London and South Western Railway produced its promotional work on the area for the pre-World War One traveller. *By the Cornish Sea and Moors: Holidays in King Arthur's Land*, gave a great deal of information offering a variety of Cheap Tickets from Waterloo, Holiday Season Tickets and a number of Two or Three Days' Tour arrangements taking in the entire area, via train and coach. Port Isaac, Tintagel and Boscastle were obvious attractions from Padstow and Wadebridge, whilst Hartland and Clovelly in Devon and, of course, Tintagel, to the south, featured prominently in facilities from Bude.

As ever, the *Homeland Handbook* captured the essential spirit and character of North Cornwall. The train journey to Padstow prepared the tourist for the area. "Sylvan Devon is left and a sterner scene reached" was one way of drawing the contrast between the two counties. 'Sterner scenes' in the more immediate environment of Bodmin Moor and its fringe land did not predominate, however, but there was no mistaking the fact that, once into North Cornwall, one was in another land, as the *Homeland Handbook* emphasised when considering Padstow:

> After quitting the train we find the approach to the town from the station a remarkable one. We walk along the stony track by the line, which is usually cumbered with tracks; between us and the river are sheds heaped with boxes, barrels and baskets, either containing fish, or intended for fish, or just emptied of fish. The notion sizes us that we are not on British ground at all but have reached some small continental seaport and are humbly progressing towards the Custom House. The fact that ere long we do pass the Custom House adds to the impression, Then we emerge upon the North Quay. The scene at high tide is pretty enough; small vessels of different builds sway against one another; there is some desultory loading and unloading going on; idlers loiter about enjoying the aspect of other people's activity, and under the hill little low buildings of a more or less maritime character are clustered together. We turn a corner to find an unpretentious post office; light upon Ye Olde Shippe Inn with carved wooden sign and antiquated air, not at all in keeping with the fact that this is a temperance hotel. It rather suggests sack or Canary, or the Jamaica rum of another time . . .
>
> . . . Narrow streets run interlaced by yet narrower ones; by and by we realise we have seen the whole of Padstow, assuredly one of the quaintest, oddest little towns in all the kingdom.

North Cornwall was important enough by 1926 to merit the introduction of the famous 'Atlantic Coast Express.' making its initial run in July 1926. This prestigious train served all the Southern Railway resorts in the west, not least Padstow and Bude. 'The ACE,' as the train became known, was much praised by S. P. Mais in his work, *My Finest Holiday*, published by the Southern in 1927. "The latest flyer of the line," was a great advertisement for North Cornwall and for the railway itself:

> All that modern engineering ingenuity can do to make fast railway travel pleasant and comfortable has been done. Long corridor coaches, luxuriantly appointed, mounted on wonderfully smooth running bogies; little shaded lights over each seat; clean and up-to-date lavatory and washing accommodation, comfortable restaurant cars with inexpensive meals efficiently served; and the whole train hauled at express speed by a monster green locomotive of 'Lord Nelson' or 'King Arthur' class – these are contribution of an enterprising railway management to your holiday pleasures.

Well before the first World War the area was attracting new residents. The small communities of Rock and Polzeath, for example, were noted for their development in the first decade or so of this century. Crossing the River Camel from Padstow to Rock, by ferry, the *Homeland Handbook* wrote for the tourist:

> Here they will find themselves in one of the many resorts that are growing up all over Cornwall, with new houses, a hotel and all the indications of being ready to welcome the expected visitor.

At nearby Polzeath and at Trevone, close to Padstow there was, similarly, the combination of magnificent coastal scenery and clear evidence of the steady growth of population and community, "well built modern houses offering accommodation and several picturesque bungalow residences." Between 1931 and 1939 Padstow's Urban District grew by 7.4 per cent and Bude and Stratton by 9.2 per cent. Elsewhere Newquay and Looe were the only similarly placed communities to show comparable growth. In every other district of North Cornwall, as in most of the county, there were, at best, only the smallest increases in population and at worst conspicuous decline, as in the Camelford Rural District at 6.8 per cent. Between 1939 and 1948 Padstow continued its growth, at 4.1 per cent and Bude at 16.1. Newquay grew at a record 32.7 per cent, and Looe at 22.9.

EN ROUTE FOR NORTH CORNWALL

THE "LORD NELSON" WITH ATLANTIC COAST EXPRESS LEAVING WATERLOO STATION FOR NORTH CORNWALL.

"ATLANTIC COAST EXPRESS"
Corridor Restaurant Car Trains will run as under:

DOWN		Up to and including JULY 9th, 1927		From JULY 11th to SEPT. 24th, 1927, inclusive	
		Every Weekday	Sats. only	Every Weekday (Except Sats.)	
LONDON (Waterloo) dep.		a.m. 11 0	a.m. 10 25	a.m. 11 10	
BUDE ... ... arr.		p.m. 4 57	p.m. 3 37	p.m. 4 42	
LAUNCESTON ... arr.		4 41	3 15	4 20	
CAMELFORD ... arr.		5 18	3 53	4 58	
(For Boscastle and Tintagel)					
PORT ISAAC ROAD arr.		5 33	4 10	5 16	
WADEBRIDGE ... arr.		5 46	4 22	5 28	
PADSTOW ... ... arr.		5 59	4 35	5 41	

UP		Up to and including JULY 9th, 1927	From JULY 11th to SEPT. 24th, 1927, inclusive
PADSTOW ... ... dep.		a.m. 8 35	a.m. 10 0
WADEBRIDGE ... dep.		8 47	10 12
PORT ISAAC ROAD dep.		9 6	10 29
CAMELFORD ... dep.		9 24	10 47
LAUNCESTON ... dep.		10 1	11 21
BUDE ... ... dep.		9 45	10 58
LONDON (Waterloo) arr.		p.m. 4 0	p.m. 5 1

Seats can be reserved on trains at 1/- per seat. For full train service throughout the day and times at other North Cornwall stations see Time Tables at S. R. Stations.

REDUCED RETURN FARES
From London (Waterloo)

To		*TOURIST		WEEK-END		† Excursion
		1st	3rd	1st	3rd	
BUDE		87/6	52/6	63/9	38/3	38/3
BOSCASTLE		94/9	58/6	70/0	43/9	—
TINTAGEL		94/9	58/6	70/0	43/9	—
CAMELFORD		90/9	54/6	66/0	39/9	39/9
PADSTOW		98/0	58/9	71/3	42/9	42/9
PORT ISAAC ROAD ...		93/3	56/0	68/0	40/9	40/9
WADEBRIDGE... ...		95/6	57/6	69/6	41/9	41/9

* Tourist Tickets issued May to October available 2 Months. Week-end Tickets, issued after 12 noon Fridays and by all Trains on Saturdays, available for return on Monday.
† 8 and 15-Day Tickets May—October on Fridays only by specified trains—see bills.

The Thirties' vogue for rambling and organised walking tours, healthy outings and being "out in the country" generally was well reflected in some of S. P. Mais' work for the Southern Railway. *Let's Get Out Here* was published in 1937 and covered rambles in many West Country settings; *Walks in North Devon, Walking at Weekends* and *Southern Rambles for Londoners* were companion volumes. *Let's Get Out Here* included a great deal on North Cornwall, particularly *Walk No. 26* (reproduced at the end of this chapter), well planned to offer up the special attraction of the Camel estuary. (The walk took in Trebetherick, beloved of Sir John Betjeman, and immortalised by the poet in the excitement and adventure of the train journey to Padstow and the long holidays by the sea.)

In the days before the onslaught of the all conquering motor-car, Camelford was something of a centre, the gateway to much of the romance of North Cornwall. Many people, it was said, got no nearer to Camelford town than the railway station, more than a mile distant. it was a "jumping off place" from which one reached Bodmin Moor – Brown Willy, its highest point, wild Rough Tor, and Dozmary Pool, the legendary scene of Arthurian romance, the lake into which Arthur's magic sword, Excalibur, was thrown. As intended, Camelford was, above all, the gateway to Tintagel, considered by many to represent the finest, most magnificent coastal setting in the county, not least, for its historical and legendary context.

One particularly inspired piece of writing on Tintagel came from the *Homeland Handbook* on Bude and its locality. In a somewhat unusual treatment, Tintagel was described in shifting perspective of distance and proximity looking to a larger context for its meaning and reference. It also offers a final, fitting testimony to all that with which the Southern Railway attempted to identify in its creation of the 'Atlantic Coast Express':

> How often have we seen it from Bude, like some vision of the land of Faerie! Nor is any of the glamour lost on nearer acquaintance. Those ruined walls are replete with poetry and romance; and dark colouring of the cliffs, their height as they rise above us, are not less impressive, forming a scene of grandeur which is in the opinion of the present writer, the finest to be found on the Cornish coast.

> There is nothing like it, perhaps in all England; for it combines natural magnificence with those traditions of poetical romance, that have for centuries influenced the life of the nation . . .

> The high road lies inland, yet as we face eastwards to return to Bude, a wide and beautiful landscape lies before us; undulating coombes that rise and fall, deepening in verdure as they roll away into Devon; and the horizon is bounded with England's strongest bulwark, the silver sea.

This was no bland promotional work. Whilst it is clearly of its own period and style, no-one could fail to appreciate its purpose, and intensity, as a visionary celebration of landscape, tradition and people. No mere description, it made for a powerful experience and image of Cornwall.

The Wondrous Coast

"DOUBTLESS," said Dr. Boteler apropos the merits of the strawberry, "God could have made a better berry, but doubtless God never did."

As good master Isaak Walton paraphrased this famous saying to uphold the merits of angling, so do I now annex it to describe my feelings after a recent visit to North Cornwall.

Doubtless God could have made a better county, but doubtless God never did.

In the first place the strangely compelling atmosphere of the Duchy begins to make itself felt almost as soon as the "ATLANTIC COAST EXPRESS" begins to leave the purple Tors of Dartmoor in the rear. At one moment you are in comfortable Devon with its terra-cotta warm loam, white cottages and thickly wooded combes, all typically English, the next you are on strange soil, suddenly thrown back five thousand years in the one British region where the successive centuries have failed to efface all trace of legend and romance. There is rich haunting music in the very place names. What play Homer and Milton, had they known of them, would have made of Tresmeer and Egloskerry, Pendoggett and Tregeargate, Roscarrock and Trevisquite, Pencarrow and Nankivell!

Long before the train has climbed the heights of Otterham the intoxicating salt-tanged air of the Atlantic, purer even than that of the Alps, has you in thrall. Shoulders are braced and eyes begin to sparkle. You have

PORT ISAAC

Going to TINTAGEL?

Travel by the "Atlantic Coast Express" to
CAMELFORD
(thence by Motor Omnibus).

CORRIDOR RESTAURANT-CAR EXPRESSES

From LONDON (Waterloo) every Week-day, 6th July to 19th September, 1931, inclusive. Seats reserved in Compartments.

To TINTAGEL.

	Atlantic Coast Exp. Sats only a.m.	R. Car London to Halwill / Atlantic Coast Exp. Not Sats. a.m.	R. Car Lon. t		Lon. to Ex. (Q. St.) a.m.	Lon. to Ex. (Q. St.) p.m.	Lon. (Q. St.) Sats. only p.m.
LONDON (Waterloo) dep.	10 24	10 40			11 0	12 40	3 0
SALISBURY ,,	12 0 noon	12 14 p.m.			12 34 p.m.	2 34	4 34
EXETER ,,	1 45	2 10			2 28	4 49	6 38
CAMELFORD arr	3 59	4 18			5 24	7 32	9 18
TINTAGEL ,,	4A30	4A48			5 A50	8A10	—

From TINTAGEL.

	R. Car Exeter (Queen St.) to London a.m.	Atlantic Coast Ex. (Q. St.) to Lon. from Hal. on Sats. a.m.		R. Car Exeter (Queen St.) to London p.m.	R. Car Exeter (Queen St.) to London p.m.
TINTAGEL dep	8A55	9A55		12 55	—
CAMELFORD ,,	9 24	10 23		1B27	3 6
EXETER ,,	12 30 p.m.	12 44 p.m.		4 28	5 53
SALISBURY ,,	2 14	2 40		6 37	8 3
LONDON (Waterloo) arr.	3 46	4 13		8 41	10 6

A—By Southern National Motor Omnibus.　　B—Change at Okehampton.

CHEAP RETURN TICKETS from LONDON to CAMELFORD

TOURIST (May—Oct.)	HOLIDAY (On various days during the Summer)	WEEK-END (Friday—Tuesday)
54/6	39/9	39/9

Take a 7-DAY "HOLIDAY SEASON"

obtainable on demand any day during the Summer at any Station shown and available for seven days, including date of issue, at all Stations between Padstow, Wadebridge, Bodmin, Camelford, Launceston, Halwill and Bude.

TRAVEL WHEN—WHERE—and AS OFTEN as you like

10/6 3rd Cl.

Children under 14 HALF-PRICE

Programmes at S.R. Stations

CHEAP DAY TICKETS from CAMELFORD
On Week-days, as under :—

Launceston	... .. 2/6	Port Isaac Road	...	1/-
Padstow	... ... 2/6	Wadebridge	...	2/-

For full details of Train Services, Cheap Tickets, etc., see announcements at local S.R. Stations, or communicate direct with the Divisional Superintendent, Queen Street Station, Exeter.

SOUTHERN RAILWAY
Quickest Way to Sunshine.

Padstow—Rock—St. Enodoc—Trebetherick—
Polzeath — Pentire Point — Hayle — The
Greenaway—The Doom Bar—Rock.

I ALWAYS like a walk that begins and ends with crossing the water.

Padstow is itself an enchanting place, but from my bedroom window I looked out over the estuary to a land of mountainous sand-dunes that looked doubly entrancing, so I decided to make my last excursion on that side.

The Padstow-Rock ferry is very convenient. It runs at all stages of the tide and every quarter of an hour. It only costs threepence. It is not surprising to find that it is well patronised.

On arrival at the other side, I climbed an Everest-like sand-dune and found myself looking down on a most attractive golf course.

I crossed this and then turned down along a lane that led to a house at the foot of Brea Hill. Just before reaching the house I took a grass-track right-handed over the shoulder of another hill, which brought me back on to the golf course immediately in front of the spire of the little church of St. Enodoc, that was formerly so deeply buried in the sand that the parson had to enter it by the roof when he could get in at all.

I saw a remarkable set of granite querns lining the churchyard. A well defined grass track led on from the church, and I took the right-hand fork which led me to a stile at the end of the golf links and so over a field on to the steep lane that climbed over Trebetherick, a quiet bay of extraordinarily well-built whitewashed houses with steep pitched slated roofs and dormer windows.

Arrived at the top of the hill, however, I was confronted by an unhappy growth of ugly bungalows, the first suburb of Polzeath, which has now grown so popular as to have become a small town.

The reason for its popularity was obvious as I came over the summit and saw the extent of its great sands, and the mesembryanthemum growing over the great caves above the pink granite rocks of Pentire-glaze.

I took off my shoes and stockings, crossed the sands to Pentire-glaze and then began an unforgettable walk all round the extreme edge of the grand promontory of Pentire Point. It was with a sense of great relief that I discovered that the whole of this peerless headland is safe for all time from the hand of the builder as it now belongs to the National Trust.

There was one place in particular that attracted me, where two men stood fishing from a flat slab below the cliffs, into a wide deep pool that seemed specially built for diving. It was so calm that a man and a girl were paddling a canoe on the surface of the open Atlantic and a dozen more were lying like seals on the pink granite rocks sun-bathing.

As I went on and upwards to conquer the top peak of Pentire the sleepers woke and raced past me to clamber up to the heights. But the headland gives no idea of the loveliness that lies beyond.

As I turned eastward beyond the point, I suddenly saw rising before me what I took to be two peaks of islands rising out of the sea. This turned out to be the peninsula of Rumps Point and Cliff Castle, where I sat for hours, glasses to my eye, watching the brown-backed guillemots swimming in line on the smooth sea below and the piping puffins darting with their absurd flappings from pillar to post.

Suddenly, over my head, quite near, I saw the upturned brown edge of the wings of a peregrine falcon. He was soon away, but it was a most fitting place for his eyrie.

Over the sea, beyond the dark cliffs of Portquin, jutted out the headland of Tintagel.

A terrifying coastline this, in bad weather, one of superb loveliness under a hot May sun. You need a whole day to take in the curves and splendours of Pentire and Cliff Castle, so I loitered here in a wilderness of wild flowers of campion and bluebell and sea-thrift, and later as I went over the fields turned in right-handed to a lane that brought me to the big square farm of Pentire, where I enjoyed a rich cream tea and had to milk my own cow for the milk.

The way on led down a daisy-carpeted path to the haven of Pentire-glaze, where I crossed Hayle Bay as it was then low tide and climbed upon the cliffs again to keep on the edge of the Greenaway and keep on the estuary edge all the way round to Trebetherick Point. Here I went down on to the sands again and kept on the sands of the Doom Bar, created in a fit of revenge by a deserted mermaid, to rejoin the ferry at Rock after one of the most enjoyable cliff walks that I can remember.

The total distance was about ten miles.

LEAVING THE FERRY AT ROCK.

AMONG THE SAND DUNES AT ROCK.

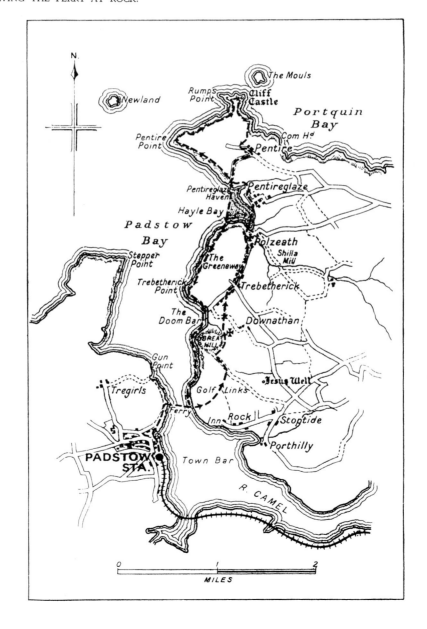

The classic post-war holiday picture. Porthminster Beach, a great favourite of people from all parts of Britain, is seen here in August 1961. This photograph captures the image and spirit of the holiday trade as it existed in what now seems more innocent times. There were to be many changes in the character of holidays and resorts during the 1960s and 1970s. This was still the English seaside holiday reigning supreme – beach huts, tea room, putting green and, of course, steam trains.

Peter Gray